S

E

The Devil & Us

A Memoir of You and Me

Paperback ISBN: 978-1-7770957-5-8

Contents

For my father

Michael Allan MacDonald

&

For my son

Brandon Michael MacDonald

Bho seo a-mach agus gu bràth bidh sinn beò gu math agus bàsaichidh sinn gu math mar a bha sinn nar triùir de chàraid foirfe.

Men's wretchedness in soothe I so deplore,
Not even I would plague the sorry creatures more.

Johann Wolfgang von Goethe — *Faust*

Foreward

If you're not familiar with Bruce's other books, then perhaps you are a little more like me. I was an ordinary skeptical person, and I've been largely asleep at the wheel for most of my life. It was only due to recent traumatic events that I earnestly began looking for spiritual answers. My world intersected with Bruce MacDonald shortly after the end of my military service where I found myself with life-threatening illness and decaying mental health. In 2022, on my knees in the shower with a razor blade at my wrist, I desperately cried out to God for help. All I wanted was to survive, and in exchange I was willing to offer any act of service — quite a childlike prayer really, and a clear indication of my economically focused spiritual immaturity, the fruit of a Catholic upbringing. My wife introduced me to Bruce via the book he wrote with John Edmonds, *Stardust Ranch: The Incredible True Story*. She said I would like him and find his story interesting. What followed was an astounding chain of synchronicity, and the first step on my new spiritual path.

A year later and after countless conversations, Bruce and I slowly got to know each other. He asked if I would like to be the editor for his new book and if I would like to meet Robert Wiegand. Having read the *Light of Darkness*, I jumped at the chance — it's not often you get the opportunity to meet people of such caliber. We all met via a Zoom call one Saturday morning, and in hindsight this meeting seemed more like a vetting process and to see if I was the right fit for the team. Bob and I gelled instantly. They both knew I was sincere, and I made it clear that my work on this project was an act of service.

In spiritual and technical terms, I am significantly under-qualified for this task and have never worked on a project like this. I'm not an editor. I don't have literary experience, and I certainly didn't have the spiritual chops to hold a candle to Bruce, or Bob. But despite my inadequacies, they both said that I was the right guy for the job. I met the challenge of this work with sincerity and a commitment to see it through. To be perfectly honest, I didn't really know what I was getting myself into. It required dedication and absolutely clean living. And lots and lots of time reading, researching and transcribing. And then there was the challenging inner-work and assimilation of new-found knowledge and a dismantling of my foundational belief systems. I totally underestimated it, and often felt like I was drinking out of a fire hydrant. I would stumble around for days in a state of confusion, moody and resistant in my disbelief. Bob would explain that I had to be fast-tracked to keep up with the book, and I am convinced that his blessings and protection were the deciding factors for success and survival. I had found a new purpose, and along with the new lifestyle, new friendships, the challenging self-examination and inner work, and the meditation, my own darkness began to lift. There were near daily meetings with Bruce and weekly meetings with Bob. They were tremendously protective and guiding forces throughout the entire project.

This work was an act of service on my behalf and an honoring of my promise to God. I didn't ask for any money. I wasn't seeking to have my name on the cover, even though it was offered many times. I've never been an editor, a researcher, a writer, or a cover designer, but I performed all of those tasks and more, in the execution of my commitment to the project. My reward has been the work, the mentoring, the friendship, and the *knowing* that somewhere, someone like you will read this and transform their spiritual life.

There were several weeks during the middle section of the book, where the experience of darkness was extremely heavy. I am familiar with PTSD and crushing anxiety and depression, but this darkness was entirely different. There were presences felt by me and my wife, including physical manifestations of knocking sounds and things being moved in the house. Our dog would bravely lead the search party to investigate the cause of these noises. At times there were smokey sulfurous odors which had no source. There were mentally visual aberrations during our deep meditations. And over the last five months, the author and I have shared many concurrent experiences. We had dreams on the same nights about demons, and our wives and extended families were spiritually bothered at the same time. There would be extended days and weeks of quiet, a surcease of botherance, and then suddenly a unified attack of sorts on all of us. Our weaknesses were probed, and our temptations arrived in unison. Our emotions and moods kept pace with the book in lock step. And there were countless synchronicities in the material we discovered whilst researching the content of these chapters. Bruce and I live on polar opposites of the globe — he in Costa Rica and me in Australia, so this was quite an astonishing phenomenon to experience when separated by such a distance. The correlation of these events would not have been possible if we had not trusted each other entirely and openly shared our thoughts and experiences. We spoke from the heart. It was not uncommon to begin our conversations with "this is going to sound crazy, but....", "hey, I had a weird dream last night". Additional to this, was the absolutely mind-boggling and uncanny way that Bruce would open lines of inquiry, share a website link from a decade ago, only to have the events unfold within days. The most profound of these, being the unfolding of the current war between Israel and Palestine.

These phenomenological experiences were not uncommon for Bruce or Bob, but they were entirely new to me and my wife. This was an undeniable experience of the spiritual realm that obliterated my skepticism. I went from believing to knowing, and that might not seem significant to you, but trust me, there is a vast difference between the two. The discomforting realization of truth and how I'd been misled, was a metaphorical unplugging from *The Matrix*. With the destruction of that chimera and its lure of blissful ignorance, came a grief for the life I once had. There were many times that I wanted to turn away and go back to my old life, plug back in, and enjoy a juicy steak. But the expansion of awareness was worth the price of admission, and I'll take clarity, truth and an honest life over deception any day.

I'm deeply grateful to Robert Wiegand and the protection, guidance and blessings we received to do this work. Adjacent to this book, Bob has been instrumental in helping me deal with PTSD. As a veteran himself, he generously offered deep insight into the condition and how to overcome past traumas, be aware of the freedom of choice, and reminded me that divine love conquers all. His perspective is truly unique, and he would often share clever metaphors to explain spiritually complex topics. He brought me to a renewed purpose and understanding that three years of psychiatric medicine and counseling could not achieve. He was, and continues to be a great friend and mentor.

Bruce and I have developed a close friendship bonded by a collective experience. We shared a psychic consciousness and quickly developed a trust to share what was going on in our lives. He has been an incredible teacher and I've been extremely fortunate to witness the process of a great writer practicing his craft. In his written work and on his podcast *MacDonald in the Morning,* he is a unique voice in the spiritual space who is clear on his message. Unlike most spiritual speakers, he pursues his work as an act of service for little to no financial gain. I've often felt that I was being water-boarded these last five months, but my spiritual growth would not have been possible without him, and I'm fortunate to have had thirty years of his life's pursuit distilled to me over five months. I'm very honored to have been introduced to his family and close network of friends. He's not bad for a Canadian.

If you live in the West, then you have been misled by the religious and political systems which govern you. You've probably experienced trauma at some point in your upbringing or adult life, and if not, then what you're about to witness in the coming years will be painful enough. Like Nora Durst from the TV series *The Leftovers,* I want to believe that I'm not surrounded by the abandoned ruin of a dead civilization. I hope this book shatters your false illusions and catalyzes you to commence, or continue, your journey of transformation and reconnection with God and divine love, because I believe that route is the only hope that humanity has. In that reconnection is healing and clarity of vision, and with your newfound sight, you will discover the subterfuge of the global narrative and the spiritual forces at play. It begins with your free choice. It begins with love and forgiveness and non-judgement. Put down the heavy family curse — it's been carried long enough. Stoke the fires of your divine light; Your ancestors, past and future are counting on it. No one else can do this for you. Thank you for your bravery in picking up this book. Don't feel alone, we are connected by purpose and spirit. May peace be with you.

Anthony Palmowski
Editor

Part I

The Devil & Me

Chapter 1

The Kill Room

Every life is a story. Time and space were created to tell stories. It matters little whether we capture these stories in tales or songs. They are captured nonetheless. They are enjoyed nonetheless, if not by we human beings upon the earth then by other beings, once human, soon to be human again, and beings elsewhere, voyeurs if you will, because the concept of privacy is the biggest joke in creation. We are all public all the time, watched by a plethora of beings who sit elsewhere, where even sit is a metaphor, for they do not have bodies and do not require the repose we require, but I have to keep the story relevant to us, and we are human beings, and therefore I personify other things like us, otherwise you might not understand them.

My family was very Roman Catholic, but it had not always been this way. Both my grandfathers had been Protestant Freemasons, blue lodge alcoholics. In my experience Freemasonry and alcoholism go hand-in-hand. I guess learning about all that rebellion against god just breaks the heart. My mother and father both chose the Catholic religion. This infuriated their fathers. My mother ended up joining a Carmelite convent. She spent a year in the convent in Kingston, Ontario. The Carmelites are a silent order. They make the Eucharist for mass. That's their holy work, that and not talking. As you might well imagine, this developed an iron will in my mother. Some stuff is so ridiculous you hesitate to even put it down on paper. It's hard to believe anybody can do these things. My mother used to flog herself before going to bed in the convent. There were whips. The nuns were encouraged to flog themselves for their sins. After a year of living in the convent my mother decided that having a family was the way she wanted to go in life. She had met my father before going into the convent, and they had gone on a couple of dates. My father was living in Montréal when he heard the news. He got in his car and drove to Kingston and proposed to my mother on the spot. They married, and I'm part of the result.

From my earliest memories, I knew that the Catholic religion was complete horseshit. As I grew into spiritual maturity over the decades, I came to realize that I was somewhat wrong about my birth religion. As a path back to god, it's complete nonsense — that part I got right. What I didn't realize was the power that this blood culture had in the consciousness of many tribes in many peoples who had been taken over by it. The blood religions have a very real multidimensional reality. It's just that they have little or nothing to do with what any reasonable person would call god.

My life story begins in the seventh month of the sixth year of the sixth decade of the twentieth century. It begins in the Ottawa General Hospital, where I, just shy of seven pounds, and yellow and jaundiced at birth, came bawling into the world. I was the second child of my mother and father. My brother had been born thirteen months earlier in the same hospital. Neither my mother nor father were born in Ottawa. My father's people, the MacDonalds came from northern Quebec, Arvida, where my grandfather worked as a foreman at Alcan Aluminum, and my mother's people, the Ross clan, came from Westmeath, Ontario, of Renfrew County.

I lived the first five years of my life in Aylmer, Quebec, in a small home near the Ottawa River. These are the earliest memories I possess. I can remember crawling on a carpet before I could speak. We are there, then we forget. It's a fully formed self, beyond even the biological personality — that comes later. The gross nature of that *created self* blocks the anterior self, and then you forget the anterior self, unless you have a near-death experience or something similar. I remember that my anterior self knew many things, that the baby body it was inside was not its first life.

I knew very early on that I had entered an extremely negative family. My anterior self would allude to it at times. It knew something. The anterior self could talk, think, reason, enjoyed attention, loved being fawned over, and was generally in love with being alive, but it also knew something dark and intense was planned for this life.

Both my mother and my father had one brother. They had this symmetry in their lives. They both disliked their brothers. We did not see much of our aunts and uncles and cousins growing up. As I grew older, I asked questions. I never got any definitive answers — *ah, Christ, that prick is a self-centered asshole,* my father would say in reference to his brother, sparing no expletive or attendant emotion, and you could see how much he felt what he was saying, and my mother would say, *well, he's just different,* in reference to her brother, and you were left to figure that out. I remember seeing *To Kill a Mockingbird* on television later in my childhood, and I thought my uncle on my mother's side must be a *Boo Bradley* type.

When I reached the age of four, my previous self faded away, making room for the current version of myself in this lifetime. However, the lasting imprint of my former self was a sense of disdain for my family. By the age of four, I wanted out. I asked my parents if I could maybe go live with my friend's family, or my junior kindergarten teacher. My mother and father found this hilarious. They tested me, dialing the number of my friend's house and handing me the phone, laughing the whole time, until I asked my question — *Mrs. Kelsoe, can I come live with you?* She could hear my parents cracking up in the background, and so she played along, asking why? I didn't have a huge vocabulary or any psychological paradigms back then, so I just said, *I don't like it here.*

My mother would grab the phone at that point and take over, saying adult things I didn't understand, and mocking me. Afterwards, I would be punished. Even at four years old, the punishment was severe and unloving. Punishment is a part of life, but outside natural law and love it's just torture, and that's what it was for me — emotional, spiritual, and physical torture. By the time I was five years old I hated my parents. I knew in my soul there was something very dark about them. It was just that my child's mind couldn't put it all together.

So what did I know? What compelled my desire to leave my family, to live elsewhere? I knew there was no love there, no real love. I knew even as a child that my mother and father were incapable of loving, but I didn't know why. Furthermore, I also knew that love was an integral part of life, and that if I was deprived of it in my formative years, I would feel the effects my whole life. How could I have known these things? I was just born knowing these things. I didn't have Carl Jung in my head explaining it to me at four years old, no complex psychological paradigms in my mind — what mind? I was four years old.

Why do we start anew with a clean slate in each reincarnation, devoid of memories? This question often arises, yet the assumption that we are completely wiped is not accurate. We're not wiped. It's in our souls. The human soul evolves to a perfection, and these souls don't need mental paradigms, just like a salmon needs no mental paradigm to find its spawning ground thousands of kilometers away. I was born knowing the power of love, and in that knowing I could see the absence of it in my family, in my mother and father. I could see the abject darkness of their existences.

Things went from bad to worse real quick. My grandfather on my father's side died when I was two years old. He was killed by cirrhosis of the liver and emphysema, and this means he slow suicided — he smoked and drank himself to death. I never really knew the guy, nor did I know how much his absence would affect me. It further isolated me inside this crazy nuclear family that had already separated itself from the only cousins I could ever know, the only aunts and uncles I could ever know, and the only recourse I had against the dictatorial isolation of my mother and father's governance of the family.

My paternal grandfather was amateur hour compared to the exit of my maternal grandfather. He went in style, the depressive alcoholic version of a Viking death. He stopped talking when I was born. He never uttered another word in his life, which would last three years. Both grandfathers were gone before I was four years old.

My maternal grandfather lived in the home in which my mother was raised. It was a small white farmhouse, wood slat exterior and a corrugated metal roof. It was two-story, wood heated, a wraparound veranda, and it had a dirt floor cellar where my grandmother kept all her jams and preserves. It had one of those pull-chain light bulbs for illumination. You had to go down a creaky set of steep wooden stairs so steep, that it sometimes felt more like a ladder than a staircase. To the side of the house, there was an unusual connecting room with a side entrance leading into it, and in one corner an old outhouse. There was a wooden plank all around the room in a horseshoe shape and three small steps that went down to the dirt ground. It was the old kill room. My grandfather used to kill a pig every fall and hang the carcass in this room because it was uninsulated and unheated and served as a freezer all through the cold winters. He also killed chickens there and the occasional lamb. There used to be a much larger barn on the property, but I never saw it. It had been taken down by the time I was born. My grandfather used to run a dairy business, and he sold milk in the small community of maybe five-hundred people. In the winters he lived in bush camps and cut wood.

In the third year of his silence, he began a communication with my grandmother, who, like the dutiful Catholic wife, had stayed by his side through all of this nonsense. My grandfather was sixty-three years old at this time. My grandmother still worked. She was a cook for a doctors' office in the nearby town of Pembroke. To the people in Westmeath it was a big city. It had a population of over thirty-thousand people. Its main industry was a big match factory, and it reeked of sulfur all the time. When I was a kid I saw the film *Shane* with Alan Ladd in the local theater for twenty-five cents. The office had three doctors and my grandmother made them breakfast, lunch, and dinner. She was renowned for her cooking. She made everything from scratch. There was nothing prepared in my grandmother's kitchen. It was flour, sugar, vegetables, spices, yeast, eggs, meats, and too many things to list here, everything you would need to maintain a perfect diet, making everything from scratch. I had never heard anybody inspect food before. People would come by my grandmother's farm with chicken or beef, and she would survey the meat like a gold assayer in a mineral office, listing all the defects and describing exactly how the meat was raised to create the defects. If a chicken had been allowed to run around too much it would have a certain flavor my grandmother could taste. It was an old-world wisdom that few people have anymore.

Pembroke was about thirty minutes away. My grandmother would get picked up every morning and dropped off in the evenings. She was gone the whole day, but it didn't bother my grandfather too much. What was he going to miss, the conversation? He hadn't uttered a word in three years. The *communication* started on a Monday. It was winter. In that part of Ontario, the sun goes down at about five pm in winter. When my grandmother came home it was pitch black. There were no streetlights in Westmeath, at least not on the little side street on which my grandmother lived. She had to trudge through the snow for about a hundred meters to get to the front door of the farmhouse. The car couldn't get her any closer because the road wasn't plowed. In the absence of recent snowfall, a well-trodden path would be visible from my grandmother's daily walks. This was the route she traversed each morning to reach the pick-up point for the car to Pembroke and retraced every night upon returning home. If there'd been snow, she'd have to form her path anew, by walking through snow that could be anywhere from her knees to her waist. Country life in Canada is no picnic.

On this particular winter night, my grandmother got out of the vehicle, said her goodbye, and thanked her friend for the ride and closed the passenger door, then watched the car drive away. When she turned her head towards the house, all the lights inside the house went out, including the porch light, everything went dark. It was like a blackout, but it was just the one house. My grandmother could see the lights in all the other houses. Slowly and carefully, she made her walk through the cold dark night to the unlit house. She could have easily hit a patch of ice on the driveway and fallen. At the door, she fumbled around inside her purse to find the house keys. The porch light usually helped with this, but it was much more difficult in the dark. When she found the keys she had to touch with her gloves off to try to identify the front door key. When she finally got the door open, the interior of the house was pitch black, no candles lit, no oil lamps, which they had for just such occasions. It had taken her nearly ten minutes to walk the hundred meters through the snow in the cold.

She called out to my grandfather. His name was Nestle. What was he going to say? He hadn't said a word for three years. My grandmother listened carefully but heard no movement in the house. She made her way to the kitchen and found the emergency candles and lit one. She then lit some oil lamps to keep the kitchen illuminated. She walked upstairs with the candle in a candleholder, checked the bedrooms, the bathroom. My grandfather was nowhere to be found. The last place that she checked was the dirt floor cellar, which also had the fuse box for the house, and there he was, sitting in the dark on a wooden chair. He had flipped the breaker. There was nothing wrong with the electrical system. She asked him why he shut the lights off. He maintained his silence, She flipped the breaker back on and all the lights came back. She went back upstairs. He ambled up some time later.

The same ritual was executed every day for five days, Monday to Friday, for that whole work week, the only variable being the proximity to the house, every day the lights waiting a little longer to go out. My grandmother became a bit frustrated and chastised my grandfather on the third day, though she was talking to a wall. He wouldn't break his silence. She couldn't figure it out. It was the simplest of symbolic language. Maybe she just didn't want to know. On the fifth day, the Friday, she was right up to the front door with the keys in the lock before the lights went out, so close to entering the house she entertained the idea that the ritual was over, but it wasn't finished yet. Its cycle of purpose had not manifested yet, close, very close, just the one last time, that Friday in 1969. On this last day she heard movement in the house after the lights went out. She heard my grandfather going up the steps from the cellar, and she heard the door at the back of the house open and close on its springs. She was fumbling around for candles, muttering his name under her breath in frustration when she heard the gunshot. He blew his head off with a ten gauge shotgun in the kill room.

The ambulance came. My grandfather lived for two more days with half a face and half a head in the hospital. My grandmother had missed the simple symbolic communication, lights out. He was going to end it. He was going to turn his lights off. I didn't hear that story till I was fifteen years old. The cover story we were given in my family was that my grandfather died of cancer. We used to visit that little town of Westmeath every summer and spend time with my grandmother, sometimes weeks on end, left without our parents, the grandchildren alone with the grandmother, and everybody in that little village, population three hundred, knew the truth except us. Every adult that passed us on the street or saw us in the corner store knew what had happened to our grandfather, and nobody told us. Everybody kept the secret. The only reason I found out is because I bought a BB gun. When my father saw it, he said I had to get rid of it. When I kicked at the idea and told him how much money I'd spent to get the BB gun from a friend, he told me the truth about my grandfather. He told me not to tell my mother that I knew.

When I was eight years old my mother wanted to go back to work. She was a registered nurse. She felt that the children were old enough. I was eight, my brother was nine, and my sister was five. My mother wanted *latchkey kids*. It's a fascinating term that originated in the seventies and eighties, specifically for my generation, *Generation X*. A significant number of my peers were raised without parents at home when they got back from school. They'd get off the school bus with a key around their neck, or a key was left under a mat, or some other way to get into the house involving a key was worked out.

It was a huge social phenomenon in the seventies and eighties. Kids today can't even understand. Every stage of the disintegration of the family has taken years of programming. It didn't happen overnight. The real campaign began with the *Baby Boomers*. They were the generation the programming forces marketed at. The idea of the individual self, and Maslow's *hierarchy of needs* as a form of self-realization in the Western model, was promulgated through television and radio and books. It was an ideological Blitzkrieg, part of second wave feminism. First wave feminism was the vote through the sufferance movement. Second wave feminism happened with the Baby Boomers after World War II.

We no longer officially have genders. I don't think we can say we're in any wave of feminism anymore, but it all began with a gender movement called feminism. Now we won't even officially define a woman — no woman no feminism. We're in uncharted waters. My mother was a relatively simple woman, no rocket scientist to be sure, raised in a rural area, and one of these oppressed women the marketing campaign was targeting. She had a degree in nursing, and she did her time at the university, and the *experts* were telling her that her children could live the way all the other children lived with no consequence. It resulted in massive fights between my mother and father. This was heaven and earth stuff, end of the world stuff.

My father wanted her to stay home a lot longer with the kids. He didn't believe in women leaving the house when they had children. This may sound sexist and antiquated to you, but look at the world now and ask yourself if he wasn't right. We have become so enamored with the concept of progress that anybody who opposes it is the modern heretic. But have you ever asked yourself what we're progressing towards? Where are we going? What is this *brave new world* and this *brave new future* for the human race beyond superstition and cultural stigmas like religion and gender and roles and function? My father felt in his gut that it was wrong. Society told us he was a *caveman*. He was against progress. My mother was all for progress. She didn't want to be trapped in a house with children. It wasn't in her. She didn't have that universal love that the universal mother was supposed to have. She'd been consuming the magazines and the television, and she'd made her decisions.

She wanted to go out into that big bad world. She wanted to *Mary Tyler Moore* the whole thing, *you're going to make it after all.* Those Madison Avenue types, who were really military intelligence types, knew exactly what they were doing. All of this has been planned.

One day in the winter a huge fight broke out between my mother and my father. It was so intense that my sister went to the basement and hid behind the furnace and my brother and I threw on our winter jackets and boots and went out to the garage and sat on top of a wood pile. We lived in the east end of Ottawa. The street I grew up on was half English and half French. The shouting and the screaming was so loud we could hear it through the walls in the garage. I was eight years old, and my brother was nine. At a certain point I just couldn't take it anymore, and I looked at my brother and I said, *I'm going in there to stop this.* He said, *don't do it.* I didn't listen to him, and I went back in the house.

I marched up the stairs and went to the master bedroom where the door had been closed. I pushed open the door. My father was in the bedroom and my mother had locked herself in the bathroom. My old man was trying to take down the door. I squared my feet and put my fists up, and I said, *if you want to fight somebody fight me.* In a millisecond I saw all the blood drain from his face. I didn't realize it back then, but I had just destroyed my father. His middle child was challenging him to a fight while he was possessed by a psychotic rage and murderous intent toward my mother. In that instant, all the tension in the room broke. My father knew he was beat. He started to leave the bedroom. He passed me without making eye contact, and I followed him out to the hallway where I watched him descend the stairs, and just before his head disappeared going down the stairs, he looked at me and said, *I was raised that a man runs the house*, then he disappeared.

My mother came out of the bathroom and gave me a hug and thanked me, but, like every cop who answers a domestic will tell you, keep one eye on the perpetrator and one eye on the victim. It wouldn't be long before my mother stabbed me in the back. After that day my old man had no use for me. Just as I had wanted to leave the house from the age of four, now my father, feeling betrayed, wanted me to leave the house, but he couldn't get out of his legal obligation because I was only eight years old. At the first sign of trouble in school or anywhere else, which was quite common given the dysfunctional home I was raised in — and my mother and father never took responsibility for it, they used it as an excuse to further deride me — my old man would say, *when you're sixteen it's legal for me to kick you out and if you don't change I'm going to kick you out*. He would repeat that like a sutra, two, three, four times a year, all the way to my sixteenth birthday in July 1982.

It wasn't just the trouble in my family, the grandfathers and my father and my mother, no, the curse in my family went much deeper than that. It was like we had been marked for misery in the world and everything that we did came with a horrible price. In the course of sponsoring new alcoholics to the Alcoholics Anonymous program, which takes place after one year of sobriety, my father undertook the practice of sponsoring people. It was difficult for me to understand this when I was young. My mother tried to explain it to me, but all I could see was my fuck up of a father, and I couldn't imagine him helping anybody because he couldn't help himself.

The big problem with the old man was his rage. That big fight between my mother and my father didn't stop anything. I guess you could say my father won that fight, because my mother did not go back to work for another five years, not until I was thirteen years old. The major change after the fight that I broke up, was my mother was no longer the focus of the old man's rage. I had volunteered to be the lightning rod. I couldn't do anything right. I started hanging around with some bad kids at school. One of them came from a divorced family, in which the mother was schizophrenic, and the other one was a full-blooded Ojibwa Indian who had been transplanted from the reserve to live with a stepfather that his mother married. The native I knew from playing hockey. The other kid wasn't in any organized sporting activities. The three of us became legend for mischief in the east end of Ottawa, and especially in the Catholic school system. They were both huge in stature. The non-native kid had a hyperactivity problem that was very severe. He had given himself three hernias before puberty, so they gave him some drugs to speed up his puberty, and I don't know what they did to this kid, but they made a Frankenstein monster out of him. The native was a mutant by birth, and had a bigger head and bigger bone structure than any human being I've ever known in my life. I was small, but remember I had those thousands of hours on a heavy bag and a speed bag and practicing boxing with my brother and other kids, and all of that had been fueled with an intensity that was the product of the simmering rage my father had transplanted into me through a psychic umbilical cord we shared until the day he died. The three of us were lethal and literally kicked the shit out of anyone who looked sideways at us. To this day, I have people who will not friend me on Facebook out of fear of the memories I generated in them before the eighth grade. I don't blame them one bit. I was a complete asshole. Maybe, through the magic of the spiritual fabric of our reality, this book will find its way into their hands, and they'll be able to understand what I was going through and find it in their hearts to forgive me.

Let me tell you a little about what it's like growing up in a family where you have one of the parents sponsoring new alcoholics. Sometimes my mother would tell us to get dressed. It didn't matter what season it was. It didn't matter what time of night it was. It didn't matter what we were doing. We asked why we had to get dressed, but my mother would just say we need to go out and there would be no more detail than that, and so we would get dressed, and we would all pile into the car, and we would go somewhere in Ottawa. This would usually end with me and my brother and sister going into another room in the house when we got there, and playing or having a TV turned on for us, or playing with the children who lived in the house. It was different every time. Sometimes the instructions were more grave when we got to the home. My mother would tell us to go to the basement and not make too much noise. I came to understand that these were the serious trips out of the house. I remember one time being down in the basement of a townhouse in Ottawa. I can't remember what section of Ottawa it was in, maybe the west end, but my sister and I were playing, and I was maybe six or seven years old. It was a big puddle we were playing in, and the light was dim in the basement, because there weren't a lot of windows. That part of the basement we were playing in was unfinished, where they kept the laundry machine and the dryer. I walked through a puddle and I thought it was water at first, but then I saw it was a big puddle of blood. I can still remember the smell of that blood. That is the most amount of human blood I have ever been around at one time. It was fresh blood, and it had the scent of copper. There was an almost mineral aroma to it, something kinetic or electrical about it. I yelled up the basement stairs, even though my mother gave me the tone of voice that said this is serious and don't bother us, but I figured a puddle of blood was serious enough to interrupt her, so I yelled up the stairs and said, *mom, there's a big puddle of blood here!* She came bolting down the stairs and turned on the light and sure enough, it was a big puddle of blood. She said something like *oh my god*, and grabbed me and my sister by the hands and pulled us upstairs and told me to take off my socks, which were covered in blood. I was never directly told, but I later figured it out as the years went by. We were playing in the exact location that the alcoholic had attempted suicide by cutting his wrists, and he had sat down there in the basement and bled out for some time until he was found. I never got a follow-up, but I'm pretty sure due to the silence in the family that the guy died. A lot of these calls were suicide attempts by addicts. Some of them lived and some of them died. This was a normal part of my life before the age of ten. My mother and father would always go together. Even though my father was the guy's sponsor in Alcoholics Anonymous, it was usually the spouse who needed consoling, and my mother would come in with her Al-Anon training and experience, and sit holding the woman's hands for quite some time at the kitchen table, while they all drank coffee and my old man chain-smoked cigarettes to the point that the whole kitchen was a blue haze.

One and a half weeks into school, in the second week of September, true to his word, the old man told me to get out of his house. At this time, I would have been about eight or nine weeks past my sixteenth birthday. The old man was just waiting for the opportunity. You might ask yourself what kind of adult human being would hold a grudge against their eight-year-old child for breaking up a fight eight years prior and then follow through on that grudge by attempting to destroy the child? The answer is my father. Unfortunately for him, he'd started training my brother and I in boxing when we were ten and eleven years old, and there was nothing he could do by the time I was sixteen. I could have knocked him out with one punch if I wanted. I'd been spending a minimum of thirty minutes a day on a heavy bag and thirty minutes on a speed bag plus skipping rope for four or five years, and to the old man's credit he was a good boxing coach. He had a whole shelf full of books, and he knew the sweet science pretty well. I was a deadly kid. When I grew up not everybody was studying mixed martial arts or some form of exotic self-defense. Not many kids could really fight. I realized I was super tough. I was knocking kids down all the time. When I told the old man I wouldn't leave the house he called the cops on me. I remember being awoken by a nightstick tapping my chest as I slept on the sofa. The cops were just doing their job. They dropped me off at a hotel that cost twenty-eight dollars and I had seventy dollars to my name, and so began my sojourn in the world.

Chapter 2

Table for One

I slept rough for a week. I slept under the cover of an outdoor playground made of wood. I snuck into a few vehicles and slept in the back of them. It was real hobo stuff. I was surprisingly unafraid. I felt like I had always been meant to live alone, like the first sixteen years of my life were fitted with training wheels. My friends were quite taken aback. Nobody really saw it coming. That's the thing about being raised in psychotic circumstances, you keep it all to yourself. Remember when we're raised, we just assume everybody else has a similar circumstance to us. Normal for a child is whatever they are presented with. Children are the easiest beings in creation to fool, and because we come into the world solely with the desire to love, people who fool us are completely corrupt, but that's something a child cannot realize. We are too pure.

I was tossed out of the house by the police in the second week of September. After a week, I had had enough of sleeping outside. It was going to get cold soon. If you know anything about Canada and you know anything about Ottawa, which is one of the coldest capitals in the world, I had about a month to get my act together and to find shelter. I went to social services. They put me in the YMCA for a few nights. I had to share my room with some guy in his forties or fifties. He was really banged up and had a hard life. I didn't need to be super perceptive to see that. After that, they found a room for me in a house. The other occupants were supposed to be coming off of heroin. They were supposed to be on a methadone program. They were in the social service system, and they had promised to get off the heroin, which is why they were given the free housing. It's really amazing how quickly you pick things up, even at sixteen years of age. They were still banging smack into their veins. The room I was put into could best be described as a large closet. It had no door. I just had a curtain that I fabricated out of a sheet I'd found. I slept on a mattress on the floor with no sheets or bedding. Here's something else people outside the drug community don't know, heroin produces bisexuality. As one junkie put it to me, *the bitch goes away*. I wasn't quite sure what he meant. I had a vague idea, but there was no way I could be certain at sixteen. I was a virgin and had no sexual experience besides groping a breast here and there.

There was another young person there around my age. She was a girl. She used to come to the room and call my name from the other side of the curtain to get my permission to enter the little closet. Her hygiene was poor, and I don't think she showered that often, but she was attractive and had very large breasts and a small waist. I think she wanted to be my girlfriend, but I couldn't be sure. I didn't know anything back then. She was always trying to touch my penis. I told her that I didn't want her to do that. She was a little confused at first. She offered herself sexually to most men, and very few turned her down. I guess the difference was that I was a boy, and not a man. She came to respect me deeply, and I used to loan my Sony Walkman to her. We became friends and looked out for each other. She always had money, and I found out later she was turning tricks on the streets of Ottawa. I caught her hanging around outside the front of strip bars a few times as I was walking around at night. She was always so happy to see me like we were family. I suppose we were family in a weird way.

I got word from my social worker that my time at this little closet room was coming to an end. Nothing in the social service systems seems to be permanent. You were always being moved around. I can't remember exactly, but I think I spent about six weeks at that little closet room with the heroin addicts and the prostitute. I had to get my shit together. This was the big leagues. I was an independent man in the world, and I had to take care of myself. My social worker had signed me up for student welfare. I was supposed to be finishing my high school certificate, but I never bothered registering in a new downtown high school. I wanted to work. I went down to the *ByWard Market* in Ottawa where all the good restaurants were. I started applying for jobs as a busboy or a dishwasher. I got work in a superb steakhouse. The salad bar was free for employees, and so every day when I would go in for my evening shift, I would load up with three plates of salad that included boiled eggs and cheese, and all kinds of vegetables. On top of that a lot of fat cat businessmen came in and took one bite out of a very expensive steak. I would grab most of those steaks up and take them home. I had never eaten so well in my life.

All of my friends were still in high school and living with their parents. I had to invent a completely new social life for myself. I was something of a novelty because I was so young, and I was on my own, but at the same time you could tell that I came from a very good family, and that I have been very well-fed, and that a lot of time and energy had been put into me as a physical being. I had good teeth, which is a sure sign that you have a dental plan, which is itself a sure sign that you come from a good background. I socialized with some waiters and bartenders from the steakhouse. They were all in their twenties and obsessed with sex and dating and relationships. I hadn't hit that part of my life yet, so it was all just alien to me. I was amiable and people liked me, so I just got along. Not a lot of people inquired as to what was going on. I found that a bit strange. Nobody was really curious what the sixteen-year-old kid was doing on the street.

This was back in 1982, way before the Internet, and so there wasn't all this social media and constant communication with people. I was really on my own, and as such I had to find ways to occupy my time. I had no television or anything to kill time. I would go to a movie from time to time, but they were expensive, and I didn't have a lot of disposable income. I spent most of my time working. I made just enough money to get by, and I developed a wicked habit of smoking hash. I smoked a half gram of hash a day. It was all the rage in Ottawa because the French loved it, and the French were close by in Hull, and they had taken over half the civil service in Ottawa due to the bilingual mandate brought in by Pierre Elliott Trudeau. I drank alcohol quite a bit as well. It was easy enough to cross the bridge over to Quebec and go to a nightclub and get served at sixteen and seventeen. The other thing I did with some regularity was knock people out. It didn't happen all the time, but I must've knocked out at least a half dozen people in the year and a half I spent living rough in Ottawa. The thousand plus hours I had spent on a heavy bag and the speed bag made me quite lethal. When you're that young and on your own, there are a lot of predators. I used to hitchhike between Ottawa and Quebec across the bridge. Every once in a while, somebody would pick you up that wanted to grab your cock. Maybe they thought I was a male prostitute. My standard procedure for that situation was to get the driver to take me a few blocks from wherever I was going, either returning to my apartment in Ottawa or to the location I was going to in Quebec, and then when we got close by, and we were at a red light waiting for it to turn, I would just knock the guy out and get out of the car. Some of these guys had gray hair, but I didn't care. If they were going to prey on a sixteen-year-old boy then they deserved to get knocked out. I never ran afoul of the police because I was not a criminal. I always worked for my rent money, and I made an honest living.

It's time now to explain more about what this story is really about. I have to get a lot of my biographical data out of the way to set up the bigger picture, which is about the karma of families and the spirituality of families, and the fact that certain family lines are cursed. I came from a cursed family line. Most of the curse came from my father's side, but some of it came from my mother's side as well. The very first apartment I found for myself was a one bedroom in downtown Ottawa. It was owned and run by a couple of alcoholic lawyers who looked to be in their early sixties, but it's hard to tell people's age when you're sixteen or seventeen years old. A lot of times I'll remember a public figure, and that will give me a gauge for the person's age, so these lawyers looked to be about the same age as Paul Newman when he made *Absence of Malice*. That's how I would explain age back then. I would say, *he looks like Paul Newman in that movie.*

My father and I had a number of physical ailments in common. There's nothing unusual about this and medicine even has a term for it. It's called congenital illness. But this was more than just congenital. When my father was a young man, he burned his feet very badly, walking barefoot through sand at a beach. The exact same thing happened to me. That's not congenital, it's circumstantial, and an alignment of circumstance that is so freakish and remote that it beleaguers the imagination. It's the kind of thing a priest or a shaman might notice. Even with all these weird little coincidences going on, my mother and father never picked up on anything. It's hard to describe how spiritually dense my family was. People think I'm exaggerating or being deliberately cruel or derogatory because I don't like them, but that's just not true. There was absolutely no culture in my family. The only thing I found even remotely classy about the old man is that he liked the singer Edith Piaf. Nobody in my family read, or if they did, it was some nonsensical biography of a political figure, or some self-made multimillionaire. The old man thought Lee Iacocca was quite something. He also considered Norman Mailer an intellectual. My mother was as dumb as a stone. She read self-help books continuously. She was enamored with Eric Fromm. I don't mean to speak negatively about my mother, but you must admit that somebody who can't see the difference and diametric opposition between the religious theology of the Catholic Church and the humanist values of this psychotherapist is kind of missing the boat, and perhaps acting in a contradictory way when they go to mass every Sunday. A lot of Catholics are like this. They make a pretense to live a spiritual life, but they're humanists and intellectuals, all the while affirming that Christ's sacrifice is guaranteeing their salvation. It's enough to make you vomit, and I could see through it by the time I was fourteen years old.

The main culture in my family when I grew up in the seventies was Alcoholics Anonymous and Al-Anon. My father went to at least three meetings a week. The family narrative is that he quit drinking when I was born. That makes two notable events, my grandfather stopping all speech and communication, and my father terminating alcohol, both at my birth. I can't even count the number of Alcoholics Anonymous meetings I've attended. It was like a form of babysitting in my family. Most of these meetings took place in church basements, and everybody drank stale coffee out of Styrofoam cups and chain-smoked. And then there were the stories themselves. They were right out of a pulp fiction novel. All these poor bastards, talking about how alcohol had ruined their lives, and taken everything they cared about away from them, but they just couldn't stop drinking until they hit rock bottom. Then came the higher power nonsense. Some higher power came into their lives and transformed them. The old man stuck at this culture his whole life and even in his mid-eighties was still going to weekly meetings. We didn't have any normal people coming over to our house for dinner when I was growing up. They were all in the program. My mother seemed to be running the whole show. I guess my grandfather had been an alcoholic who had never hit rock bottom. If she couldn't control her father, she sure as hell was going to control her husband. It was the most basic of psychodramas.

Literally, everybody who came to our home was an alcoholic. There were no exceptions to this rule. It was like a cult. We were not deprived of the various professions and personalities in our social life. There were alcoholic doctors, alcoholic lawyers, alcoholic Catholic priests, just about any profession you can imagine had alcoholics. It was like my mother wanted us to know that this was a disease, and it affected all kinds of people in various sectors of society. The disease took her father. The disease was in her husband, but she was going to save him. When we were twelve or thirteen years old, my mother suggested that we go to Alateen. My brother and I wanted nothing to do with it. My sister became involved in her late teens. She went to a group called adult children of alcoholics. She claimed to get a lot out of it, but she's been as crazy as a shit house rat her whole life. She also inherited my mother's outrageous pretense at normalcy. Crazy people may as well wear a hat that says *I'm crazy*. They go to such lengths to pretend they're normal. They like to dominate and direct conversation in social situations, less they be directed to a place that exposes them as completely crazy. Once you know what to look for you can see them a thousand meters away.

My brother focused on getting everything right. He did very well at school and got good grades, but not because he understood the subject, rather because he had an excellent memory and would do excessive study forty-eight hours leading up to the semester exam. He excelled at sports, and we both played competitive hockey for over a decade. I have to give the old man his due. He was extremely diligent with getting up in the morning and going to the practices and going to the hockey games on the weekends. The other fathers on my hockey team and my brother's hockey team were the only non-alcoholic people he associated with. They sat in the stands during a practice or a game and shot the shit and chain-smoked. He physically showed up for the role of being a father, but he never emotionally or spiritually showed up. He just wasn't there. He was the man who wasn't there.

The thing about this apartment is I ended up moving into the exact apartment in which I was conceived. That is beyond all probability. If you know anyone who uses the word *coincidence* and believes it, realize you have an idiot in your life. The first rule of spiritual maturation is that there is no such thing as coincidence. For the sake of the thickheaded, I'll go through some statistics. Ottawa is not a mega-city, but it's not a town or a village either. At any given time, there must be fifty to one-hundred thousand rental units on the market. The probability that I would end up leasing the first apartment my mother and father leased in Ottawa after my mother left the Catholic convent is next to impossible when viewed through the lens of chance. My mother and father didn't make anything of it when they heard. Don't ask me to explain it yet – we're not at that part of the story. Be patient.

My hashish habit did not abate in the least. I worked and I got high. There is something quite invigorating about being that free at that age. I saw so much about what was really going on in the world. I felt like an alien visiting from another planet. I somehow knew to stay out of everything. The only thing I allowed myself was the beer and the hash. Just about everything was offered to me, harder drugs, lots of sex, and strange friendships made with people unhitched from society, people who seem to just wander the world like ghosts. I kept to myself for the most part. I hadn't seen the movie at this age yet, but later on I would see it — I was a little like Travis Bickle in *Taxi Driver*, wandering the streets at night, observing everything around me, an internal monologue documenting everything, except, unlike Bickle, I didn't want to clean the city up. I wasn't waiting for *a real rain to fall and wash all the scum away*.

People who run things are very seedy. I imagine all capital cities are cesspools. Ottawa was no exception. It had a huge gay community made up of men in marriages with children. I'm not even sure gay is the right word. It seems derogatory towards gay people. To me a gay man is somebody who is born polarized toward the feminine and attracted to the same sex. What I was seeing in Ottawa at night was just sex for the sake of sex without any heterosexual or homosexual attributes. It was just men looking to get off.

My father had told me that Pierre Elliott Trudeau was like this, a sex freak who would lie down with almost anybody. The old man worked for external affairs, which was the old name for the ministry that is like a state department in the United States. State departments or their equivalent ministries in the Commonwealth countries had two main divisions, diplomatic and economic. My old man was an economist. He had been around the world six times if you added up all his air miles. He was functionally intelligent. So am I, if the truth be told, but I have more creative intelligence than my parents did. It's what set me apart in the family and made me an outcast. My brother and my father were wicked-smart in the ability to learn something through memorization and they presented very well socially. But they were really shallow. They were like a foreshadowing of something that would become hyper-popular in the world, artificial intelligence, except it's the opposite of what everybody thinks. It's not machines learning to think like human beings, it's human beings learning to perform like machines. Inversion is a huge part of the story I'm going to tell, so pay attention.

The old man had been everywhere. He had seen the dead cart in India, which is a mule or oxen pulled cart that goes around in the morning with a guy ringing a bell, and everybody brings out their dead bodies, the family members who died in the night. The dead cart took them off to the cremation grounds. The old man had seen men beheaded on the beach in Saudi Arabia, and he had been on tours of the worst prisons in Turkey and had seen a penis cut off by an inmate and kept in a formaldehyde jar in a storage room in the prison. The prisoner felt that his penis had ruined his life, so he cut it off in solitary confinement. The old man didn't even realize what he was doing. He was prompting a curiosity in me to go out and live my own life and have my own experiences. In the first eight or ten years of my life, the old man traveled so much he was gone at least a third of the year. It sort of astounded me that the government would invest so much responsibility in a moron like my old man.

This was back in the seventies, and even back then you could see the etchings of globalization. The main driving force in the ministry of external affairs was trade relationships with foreign countries, and it was all leading up to free trade. Whatever is running this world plans decades in advance, if not centuries. I apologize if that sounds conspiratorial; I was going to wait until the middle part of the book to get into the esoteric underbelly of our reality. The old man had seen his share of the dark reality of our world, both in his own soul and his own behavior through alcoholism and through his work, which took them into these dark parts of the world to see things which very few people would ever have an opportunity to see. He was so eager to keep me away from the darkness that he actually pushed me towards it. Kids will do almost the exact opposite of what you tell them. The law of inversion is not just an operating principle of the cults and sects that run this world, it's embedded in our consciousness. It has to do with the artificiality of this material plane and the way the projection mechanism creates reality in our hologram, but, like I said, the first part of the book is just the biographical information. The middle part is where we're going to get into this underbelly.

You need a physical description of the old man. He was a small man with a large stomach. His skin was yellow and jaundiced from liver damage, even though he quit drinking at thirty-one years of age. He estimates he was an alcoholic at thirteen years of age in northern Quebec. I know people who have been drinking their whole life at least three or four nights a week, and they're nowhere near as far gone physically as my old man was in his early thirties. Half of his teeth were false. He kept them in a glass of water beside the bed when he slept. This all seemed normal to me as a kid, even though my friends didn't have fathers like mine. I never thought to ask the old man or my mother why he was so banged up. To the day he died, I didn't know a thing about my father before the age of thirty-one when he quit drinking. My mother and father could keep secrets. I think it's part of Catholic culture. Maybe it has something to do with the shame of the devil in your life. Despite working at a high-level in the government as a trade negotiator and an economist, my father's physical appearance was like a man who had been in and out of jail as a bank robber in south Boston. In the church basements where he spent most of his social life at Alcoholics Anonymous meetings he looked normal.

Chapter 3

Forty

After I was kicked out, there was not a lot of communication between myself and my family. My mother felt that my father had gone too far. But it didn't matter because I actually liked being on my own. I embraced my life as a moment-by-moment occurrence, and I embraced the fears that came with being alone and unprotected in the world. The truth is, I had never felt so alive in my life. Lines were crossed in the decision which my father made in that fall of 1982. The old man was an ultimatum guy. He had spent his entire adult life in the foreign policy division of a national government. I think part of him wanted to make the tough decisions that he saw other people make. I think in his own stupid way, he was trying to pantomime people like Henry Kissinger. He was practicing bitter medicine for better results. My father actually believed a lot of the bullshit that was printed in newspapers in foreign-policy rags. In his defense, the idea that a lot of these people were psychotic — and perhaps demonically possessed — had not really become topical in society yet. If you have not figured it out yet, then, let me just tell you straight up — Henry Kissinger was a complete psychotic, and if he was not demonically possessed, then he was living proof that the human is a class of being more vile than the class of demons. Maybe the creator didn't set it up this way, but never underestimate the growth potential of human beings. We've grown into our wickedness.

After a decade and a half of sobriety, and to be fair to the old man, countless sponsorships of new people in the program of Alcoholics Anonymous, he had developed what Sigmund Freud, another demon in the flesh, called the *superego*. The old man was in love with himself, and because his cosmology was Catholic, everything was run through this ridiculous cosmic philosophy. The superego is a concept coming out of the Abrahamic religions. I am damn near sure that in my old man's twisted head, he saw what he did to me as the same test god put Abraham through with the sacrifice of his son. Except the Bible gives no indication that Abraham was an addict and abusive to the people in his family, minus the attempted murder of his own son, of course.

There are a lot of people who tell us that the Bible is being frequently misinterpreted, particularly in instances where figures like Abraham are criticized for obeying god's command to sacrifice his son. They tell us that the Bible is a layered and encrypted and occulted narrative and needs to be rendered by someone with the authority to do it. That's true, and I have no disagreement with it. The problem is when you truly decrypt it and reveal the multidimensional nature of it, it's even creepier than the literal. But we'll get to that in the body of the book.

A human being can live within an impulsive moment of fight or flight for only so long. If it becomes normal, the brain does not form correctly. I had been living in this hyper-fueled way for well over a year. I worked in restaurants in the winter, and I got construction jobs in the summer. The construction paid much better, and I liked to stay strong. The physical work helped develop my body and my overall strength. I did what I wanted when I wanted. I found some roommates to move in with me and the rent was split a few ways, so I had a little more spending money. I was still smoking hash every day.

People do what they do because they want to do it. People who drink every day and get really drunk do it because they want to do it. I smoked hash every day because I wanted to do it. It became a major part of my culture. All my friends smoked hash. I liked the feeling of being high on THC. There was nothing going on in my life that necessitated I do not get high every evening. This was perhaps the biggest lesson of that year that I lived alone after being ejected from my family home. A life needs a purpose. Everything that comes into existence has a purpose. A snake's purpose is to control the population of the things within its food chain. If the snakes didn't show up for work, we'd have serious problems. A tree's purpose is to consume carbon exhaled by us and produce oxygen. If the trees didn't show up for work every day we'd be in serious trouble. I became acutely aware of this in the year which I had been on my own. I started to wonder what my purpose was. It seemed ridiculous to me that all there was to life was showing up for work and then coming home and getting high. I was barely into my seventeenth year, and I could figure that out. But what was it? I started to study people a little older than me quite closely. I got into long conversations with the waiters and bartenders at the steakhouse. I asked them what they were doing with their lives. I got fairly honest and open answers from everybody. There was one fellow who was in law school. He had to wait tables to supplement his student loans. He was married, but he didn't have any children yet. Other people were doing graduate work at Ottawa University or Carlton University. Nobody was just a bartender or just a waiter. I didn't want to be just a dishwasher and just a busboy. I began to think long and hard about this.

I didn't realize it back then, but I was extremely comfortable with darkness. Most people would be nearly suicidal with the level of despair I experienced. I had been ejected from a middle-class life and thrown to the streets, but I never felt more alive and more purposeful in my survival. There was a cocoon of darkness around me. Darkness is a protective force. It has been greatly maligned. People don't really understand darkness. It's really a spiritual force that operates at one end of the spectrum. On the light end you have living *in the moment*, the only real thing. Darkness does the same thing. It keeps you *in the moment* because survival and god are the same thing. This is the truth about darkness. It's the people in the middle who are the dead weight in the human experience. They neither pursue the light nor fear the dark. Circumstance has created this buffer that was never meant to exist. The people in the middle are the scum of the earth. All the scheming is done by the people in the middle. The people in the moments of light or darkness cannot scheme. The moment allows no scheming. It's the practice of conjurers. They want to conjure the moment just after this one. They want to control it. And the moment after that as well.

In time, my moment of darkness passed, and I started to contemplate my life again. It was nearly a full year of living as though tomorrow didn't exist until it manifested. I didn't realize it at the time, but I had taught myself to live spiritually, to live in the moment, and it had ruined me for anything else, and the world we created in the twentieth century is nothing other than this middle place, this other place outside of life, this pretend life, this go-to-sleep life where people went to die while their bodies kept walking. I could see it so clearly. It made me sick. By the time I was seventeen years old, people were pathetic to me, incapable of living, afraid of the gift of life. The primal urgency of darkness was gone, and the conscious pursuit of light had disappeared in the West. We were a pathetic people. I could see it so clearly way back then in 1983. There was no going back for me.

Unknown to me at the time, my realization had brought something into my timeline. It happened this way. Part of my job at the steakhouse was washing the cloth napkins. This was done at a laundromat down the road from the steakhouse. I had to walk over with a giant bag of napkins slung over my shoulder like jolly old Santa Claus. One day, I threw all the napkins into three machines. I couldn't really leave the laundromat once the washing process had begun. The chances that someone was going to steal wet cloth napkins was slim, but they were my responsibility. That's the way life works. So, I just sat there on this crappy little metal leg chair, the kind you might find outside a principal's office in a high school, the gallows chairs, where the delinquent would wait to be disciplined by the vice-principal. I left the laundromat to smoke, but I stood right in front and watched my machines. When the wash cycle was over, I moved everything to the dryers. I had a pocket full of quarters that my manager at the steakhouse had given me. On one of my trips out front to smoke a cigarette, I saw a poster on a cork-board, you know, one of those public announcement cork boards in a laundromat — missing cats, roommates wanted, bicycle for sale

— and there was this one-page flyer on meditation. I don't know why it stood out. It just did. It said newcomers were welcome, and that meditation could be learned by anybody, and that extraordinary benefits could be had by regular practice. It hinted at something. I didn't know what it was hinting at back then, but that's the point of a hint, to keep you moving in a certain direction. I noted the address and the time for the open house, and I committed to going. I had that night off work, and I was able to attend. I was still smoking hash every day, and I was still knocking out the occasional idiot on the street, but I wanted to learn how to meditate.

It occurred to me, as I was working on this manuscript, that some forty years — almost to the day — had passed since that fateful day I had seen the foolscap tacked to the corkboard inside the laundromat in the ByWard Market of Ottawa. Now, I certainly do not advocate the study of numbers to comprehend reality. The secret societies call it numerology. Gematria is a bit different and correlates numbers and letters to divine a code, and it can, and often does, induce madness because human beings are not computers. And with that missive given and that caution passed, I will take a moment to explain the significance of the number forty as I have come to understand it through epiphanies, as revelation is the divine process and calculation is the demonic process. The number forty is one moon plus twelve. A moon is twenty-eight days. If you take the sum of forty and divide it by twelve you come to three decimal three repeating. Anywhere a number cannot close — these nonclosures are always of an ordination of three, whether it be three repeating or six repeating or nine repeating — it signifies a gateway in reality in which the god energy comes. Everything else is closed and fixed, and this is what we call the machination of fate. It is true that much of the universe can be understood by math, but it produces a human being we will explore more fully in the body of this book. Our way out of this reality into the super-reality is through the heart, not the head. We're not computers.

I went on the appointed day to the appointed place and there was a small group of maybe fourteen people. They were all adults. I was just past my seventeenth birthday. I guess you could say I was still a minor. I was not a legal adult, but I was legal in the sense that I was living on my own and paying my rent and keeping a roof over my head. I got a few glances as I walked into the small, rented space, which, had it not been the space of this spiritual group, might have been a bookkeeper's office, just a small commercial space suitable for the gathering of people.

Back then I guess you could say I dressed like a thug. I still had a baby face, as my beard had not come in any significant way. I wonder what they made of me. I was warmly greeted. I told them that I saw their flyer in the laundromat and that I wanted to learn more. We had a short meeting of about forty-five minutes in which the basic philosophy of meditation and the *inner life* was explained, and I won't go into any detail on this particular path because they're all basically the same, and then the rudimentary explanation of meditation was given. That was it. There was no book to take home. There was no money to pay. There was nothing asked of me. It was exactly as advertised. Learn how to meditate.

I went home and tried the technique immediately. I don't know if it had something to do with the earnestness of my youth or the literalness of my mind at that time, but my very first time sitting and straightening my spine and concentrating on my forehead as I was instructed to do, popped me right out of my body. I was up in the corner of the main room in the very apartment in which I was conceived, looking down upon my body, which sat cross-legged on the floor. I couldn't believe it. I was so stunned I popped back into my body almost immediately. Then came the great fight with my mind: *That didn't really happen. You were not just up in the corner of the room looking at your body.* Another voice inside me said, *yes I was*. This is exactly what I was told might happen in the meditation technique. Well that was it for me. I was hooked. Thirty minutes of meditation achieved what sixteen years of Catholic indoctrination could not. I was absolutely fascinated by the inner life. The difference was that my new inner life was phenomenological. There was nothing to believe, whereas all my Catholic faith was just that, faith.

On that one fateful day, after following through on the advertisement on the corkboard in the laundromat, and learning how to meditate, my entire life line was changed. People usually apply great importance to events like this. If this were the biography of a yogi, I might be describing the moment I realized I had done all this before in a previous life, but this isn't the biography of a yogi. This is the story of a Scottish Canadian raised Catholic in an alcoholic home who learned to meditate and popped out of his body the first time he tried the meditation technique. Nothing more and nothing less.

What happened next was a transformation of my life. I can't overstate the significance and the importance of that meditation experience. It was not easy to replicate. In fact, it was sometime later that I was able to get out of my body again. The general meditation technique proved to me that we were something more than just this body. The key word here is *proved*. It's very important that the spiritual life be proved. This does not mean that there's going to be a consensus in society, and the reason for that is that we are all at different levels of spiritual evolution. There is a *continuum* down here, for lack of a better word. Some people are farther down the continuum than others. You can read this to mean some have had more lives. You can read this to mean that they've been down here longer. The process is generally the same for everybody. There are no exceptions. But to really begin a spiritual life you must have something proved to you. If all you're going on is faith, then you're not going to have very much of a spiritual life, and you're going to be plagued by doubts and, even worse than that, you're going to develop the absolute opposite of what your spiritual life was intended to create.

There are natural operative laws down here that when violated create consequences. The concept of god has become the hallowed ground of the most sociopathic personalities in the human record. After all, what could be more important than to be the voice of god? Once you understand what a sociopathic personality is, the rest becomes fairly easy to put together. I began to meditate regularly. I meditated every day. I quit smoking hash. I quit drinking beer. Nobody told me to do these things. I wanted to become better at meditation. I had the general lingering idea that purity of mind and body was an aid to meditation. I was not incorrect.

I would like to tell you that there was some great reconciliation with my family, but the opposite was true. My spiritual development was further cause to separate myself from them. I began to have profound intuitive senses about a lingering evil in my home and in my bloodline. I had no mental concept or mental understanding of what was going on in my family, but, at an intuitive level, I just knew to stay away. It was like the meditation gave me a fuller understanding of the four-year-old boy who wanted to leave the home, although I still had no full idea of what the real reason was. There is a season for everything in life and patience is absolutely required to unfold properly. Meditation teaches patience.

I began to study literally everything I could get my hands on as it related to consciousness. I started to read everything about the eastern paths and meditation. Now remember, this was back in 1983, so there was no internet. Everything had to be done the old-fashioned way. I started spending a lot of time in libraries. I wasn't that far from the main library in downtown Ottawa, and I started going quite regularly. I didn't get a card and start checking books out, but I did spend a lot of time in the library with books and reading. I became fascinated with poetry. I remember my favorite poets being Ted Hughes and Wallace Stevens, and to a lesser extent Charles Olson and Philip Larkin. I had absolutely no idea what drew me to a poet. I had no background in poetry. I had no understanding of the musicality of poetry. I didn't understand what an iambic pentameter was. I didn't understand what free verse was. I just found it fascinating when Ted Hughes said that *a pebble was imprisoned like nothing else in this universe*.

It was like a whole other Bruce was born. I don't mind telling you that I took a bit of a victory lap as it concerned my family. I seemed to have some form of confirmation that I was never meant to be born in that family, although I was born in that family, so fate would contradict me and, in this regard and in all regards, fate is always correct. Our lives unfold because they have been structured. We are actually architects of our lives. This all takes place before we are born. The entire concept of a human life is like a game. It's planned by a spirit that forgets what physical pain and physical deprivation and loneliness and spiritual isolation are all about. And in that smugness, we plan all kinds of adventures for ourselves that we immediately regret when we come wailing out of our mother's bellies.

I have to move more quickly now. As much as this may seem like a biographical book, it isn't. It's the story of us. It's the story of the West in particular, and it's the story of the world to a lesser degree, as the West is largely responsible for bringing us to the point we're at now. After being expelled from four different high schools, I discovered that my mind was now ignited in a way it had never been before in my life. Thinking and researching seemed purposeful to me. It had a purpose that came deep from my heart. It wasn't connected to just making a living and fitting into this bullshit society. I decided that I had outgrown Ottawa. I set my sights on Toronto. One summer day, I packed up all my life's belongings into one small duffel bag and got on a Greyhound bus and arrived in downtown Toronto in 1985 at the age of nineteen.

I ended up taking a room in a well-known community in the west end of Toronto, called Parkdale. I'm not going to say a lot about that because the first year of my life in Toronto has been well documented in a literary novel I published in 2007, titled *Courerus De Bois*, and republished as *God is an Economist*.

In Toronto, I worked at restaurants as a waiter because I was now of legal age to serve alcohol. To everybody who met me I was a well-mannered and well-educated young man from Ottawa who nobody could believe had spent a significant time on the street, and nobody could believe the rage that was inside me when unleashed in violence and resulting in an adult male being unconscious before me. It happened from time to time that I had to throw somebody out of the bar or smack them around and people who knew me and worked with me would become stunned. I was perceived as bookish and shy because I had retreated into myself as a meditator and as a reader, but when violence was called for I dispatched it with stunning acumen.

When I wasn't working, I sat at home in my attic room reading. I started to go through all the great literature of the world. I favored the twentieth century. I was not, at that age, quite ready for the centuries proceeding the Industrial Revolution and modernism and postmodernism. My literary period was book ended between Joseph Conrad's *Heart of Darkness* and the contemporary novels of John Updike. I particularly liked Faulkner and Hemingway. *The Sound and the Fury* seemed like a living document to me. I had never before read a book that seemed spiritually alive. Somehow Faulkner was able to make the words breathe on the page. I had never before read an author who could capture spirit and trap it in pages for future generations.

My attic room had a large closet. I would go inside the closet and close the door and meditate in there. I had no spiritual companionship. I was not a part of any group or religion. I had no interest in becoming part of any group or religion or going to an ashram or anything like that. I was just fascinated with the inner life. I remember coming out of that closet on occasions in the mid-eighties and having some new insight that beguiled me, like time doesn't exist. I would go into that attic closet for an hour and come out and say out loud, *time doesn't exist*. I didn't know how I knew that. There was no way for me to deconstruct it or prove it mathematically. I just knew. I couldn't always remember what happened to me in meditation. I would just go into a meditation and come out, and I would know something that I didn't know before I began the meditation, and I would have no line of deductive reasoning explaining how I knew what I knew. I started working on my first book. It would not be published until twenty-two years later. I wrote every day. I went to a second-hand store in Parkdale and bought a manual typewriter. I went to a copy shop and bought a bundle of paper. I continued to work construction in the summers in Toronto.

I set my sights on school and applied for Carlton University in my hometown of Ottawa as a mature student when I was twenty years old, anticipating acceptance when I was twenty-one. This was because at that age, no high school diploma was required and an opportunity to study would be given under the designation of mature student. I was accepted into Carlton University and returned to Ottawa where I rented an apartment and continued to live separate from my family. I paid my own tuition and asked nothing of my mother and father. I interacted with them socially and visited them at my family home from time to time, but our relationship was still remarkably strained. There had been no real apology to me or no real discussion of what had happened in my upbringing or my eviction from the home. My self-respect demanded that I not concede my position and become the apologetic and repentant son because I didn't believe I did anything wrong. My old man was equally obstinate, and my mother became increasingly removed. I scored remarkably well that year at Carlton University. With the marks I acquired, I applied to the journalism program at Carlton and the journalism program at Ryerson University in Toronto. The name of Ryerson University has changed as of the writing of this manuscript, but I refuse to use the new name because it's ridiculous and done under the auspices of this rabid political correctness and social transformation that is gripping the largely possessed population. Carlton rejected me. Ryerson invited me to Toronto to sit for three hours in a room with other candidates and write a spontaneous essay on why I wanted to study journalism. I went and wrote on a manual typewriter and told them a bit about my life and what I had seen and why I wanted to share the world I had seen with other people. I was accepted.

I enjoyed university immensely. I was ready to take my mental life much more seriously. I studied hard and got good marks. My best courses were micro and macroeconomics, where I scored at the very top of my year. This was no doubt the result of listening to the old man at the dinner table as he discussed global economics and social policy. It was a remarkable time to be in university because so much happened in the world. The Berlin Wall came down. Nelson Mandela was released from prison and the apartheid movement became the African National Congress and took control of South Africa. My entire university years were during the term of George Bush Senior. During this time my father was instrumental on the Canadian side of negotiating the first free trade deal.

It was a point of constant argument between us. There was hardly a dinner that could be had with me visiting the family that did not erupt into an economic argument. I was perceived as the radical liberal outcast in the family, given that I was getting a journalism degree. My brother had opted for a commerce degree at Ottawa University. It wasn't that my family was conservative or liberal. They were just stupid. I know this sounds harsh. I do love them. You cannot stop love for your blood. But you can keep your distance.

I tried to point out to the old man that if manufacturing left

Canada there would be no net benefit in the free trade deal. I pointed out to him that most of the industry in the United States was more competitive and would wipe out numerous industries within Canada. The old man would have me believe that this was an economy of scale that would lower consumer prices for everybody. My point was that there would be no consumers if people didn't have good employment by which to buy things. To this day I never really determined whether my old man really believed what he was saying or he had just been indoctrinated by his career and the social pressures of the environment in which he lived and worked. He didn't have much of a conscience. The only sympathy he seemed to exhibit for anybody were the poor slobs who ended up in the church basements at the Alcoholics Anonymous meetings. Like most Catholics, he had developed a cruelty that sought to become the manifestation of god's punishment by their indifference and callousness toward other people. I know I'm not characterizing all Catholics, but a significant portion of them are like this. If you don't see god come down and dole out the punishment then you become the instrument of god's punishment because it's the build-up pressure of deprivation from trying to live a moral life without any of the spiritual reward, and I have never met an enlightened Catholic.

I kept my spiritual life to myself. My parents knew that I had learned to meditate. I tried discussing a few of the experiences I had had in meditation and altered states of consciousness with my mother, and she immediately jumped to schizophrenia. I guess the Royal Ottawa Hospital had done to her what the Ministry of External Affairs had done to my old man. That was the end of my spiritual sharing with the former cloistered nun who flogged herself every night with a cat of nine tails. I became increasingly aware of a lingering darkness in my family that was not the imagination of a four-year-old child or an eight-year-old child or the sixteen-year-old who had been ejected from the house. It was there and it was palpable.

Alongside my contemplative life, I was beginning to stockpile a number of experiences that showed me the multidimensionality of life. I had an encounter with the dead stepbrother of a girlfriend over a three-day vacation at an isolated cottage in Georgian Bay. I brought back information to the mother and father of my girlfriend that was vetted as being accurate and would have been incapable of being in my possession had I not actually communicated with the deceased stepson, who had committed suicide by driving his automobile off a cliff in the British Columbia interior, his girlfriend in the passenger seat who he took with him to the other side of life. I was surprisingly disciplined in my spiritual practice. Even a ghost encounter did not make me want to go into the occult or the paranormal deliberately. Some steadying voice inside me kept me on the path of continual unfolding to the center of creation that we call universal love. I suspect that this was my greatest need, love. I had no room for the meandering curiosity of a spiritual peccadillo. In a way the foundation of Catholicism grounded me. I was then and still am to this day, greatly moved by the Gospels, though I can find little merit in salvation doctrine, nor am I overly impressed with the resurrection. Many of the aspects of the Abrahamic religions are nonsensical, and in total they produce much more harm than good. I took things as they came and many things came. I never sought to repeat or master one aspect of the multidimensional reality. I find psychics and readers preposterous people. For me the practice was the pleasure.

I became increasingly aware of a guiding hand in my life. It had no personality or presence. It wasn't what I would call a guardian angel. Nor would I call it a spirit guide as the new age folks are fond of as a term. It was just this growing awareness that there was an orchestrator in my life and a musicality to the circumstance and unfolding of my life. It was gentle and it was non-intrusive. The only time I got myself into trouble, is when I got myself into trouble. Regular spiritual practice does not produce a saint. It simply produces somebody unfolding toward a higher state of consciousness. I made crippling mistakes in my life that cost me years to recover from, but those very same mistakes became my greatest teachers. I also became aware of the fact that the darkness that was in my family was in me as well. If provoked or left unchecked with regular spiritual practice it could appear suddenly like mold in the rain season. I had a ferocious anger. I could destroy a person with just a few sentences by just going to the core of their being, their very weakness, and holding it in front of them in my hand. It was a horrible and dark talent, learned from my mother and father, who had it in spades. The violence abated in my early twenties, except for one incident in Vancouver in which I had to knock out two guys who tried to mug me at three o'clock in the morning, but I don't consider that the violence and rage that attended my life on the street in Ottawa.

Upon finishing my degree, I made my way out west to Vancouver for no particular reason other than my sister lived there. I had a half-finished manuscript with me and no desire to work except sustenance work in a bar, which I found at a seedy place called *The Marble Arch*, a gentleman's club that found its way into a Motley Crue song called *Girls Girls Girls*. After a short time in Vancouver the desire to move on and consume experience came upon me. I hopped on a plane and found myself in Taiwan where I taught English for two years and learned how to speak Mandarin. I was fascinated by this culture. It was otherworldly. I developed a good reputation as a private tutor for corporate types. My comprehension of the English language and its rhetoric and grammar were second to none in the class of people who went over there to teach English. I consumed every piece of Chinese scripture I could get my hands on. I read most of the sutras of the Buddha. I read the entire Taoist canon. I befriended and took counsel with an esoteric Buddhist master and a northern Taoist master. The Buddhist master read my aura and said "you are blue I can speak to you". The Taoist master helped me understand many things in the texts. I sent my manuscript home to a friend I had made at university, and she had contacts in the film industry and there was talk of me getting an agent and maybe getting this book published. I hopped on a plane to return to Canada with every intent of returning to Taiwan, where I imagined after two years, I was going to make my life, but that never happened. Life got in the way.

I met the mother of my son and got married and divorced after five years but stayed diligently attached to the role of father. I raised my son in the City of Mississauga, and while there I befriended a Sufi sheik and danced and prayed with the Sufis for over a year, all the while maintaining my core spiritual discipline of meditation. When my son finished high school, I made my second stab at being an immigrant and moved to Central America where my son and I built a series of earthbag buildings in a remote rainforest area next to a native reserve. And here I got married again to a local Costa Rican lady, born and raised on this mountain, which didn't have electricity until 2014, and I took on the responsibility of her and her family and her son, who was already an adult, and found for myself the family I could never have found in Canada.

And that's about the whole story of my life in brief. So why have I bothered to tell you my story? There's this idea in mysticism that everything is the same thing. It's universal. The mystics have been giving us the same message since the beginning of time. Everything is everything. There's a cosmic connection between a grain of sand on a beach in Guanacaste, Costa Rica, and a speck of stardust in the Milky Way galaxy. If that's true, then an advanced being could meet a typical member of western society in the twentieth or early twenty-first century and make conclusions about the entire generation. Those conclusions would be based upon a universal understanding of what a human being is, and what human behavior is, and how that behavior is expressed or not expressed in the time period denoted, in this case, the span of my life, which is now just shy of six decades. Every action and consequence in that life would be a detail in this cosmic story, and it would have to be a cosmic story, because the mystics tell us that everything is everything and everything is connected. If this is true, then a single human life properly examined is the life of a time.

Many people have an idea that we live in a very special time. If you look at the Industrial Revolution and the advancements that the human race has made, the case could competently be presented to a reasonable jury of our peers. We seem to be on the cusp of everything. We seem to have finally extorted all the truth out of our reality, which has been mute for millennia, according to our historians. We started it with calculus and physics. Super computers came in and finished the job. Now we know almost everything if you believe what the scientists are saying. We have absolutely ghoulish figures on the world stage who are telling us that consciousness can be hacked like a computer because humans are an organic machine. We're no different from the silicon machines they want to host with dislocated consciousness. It's just that we're carbon based and the computers are silicon based. But they have figured out the overall system so that it doesn't matter.

We have an increasingly panicked and disenfranchised religious community in the West that is telling us that demons are everywhere, and Satan is taking over. If you were to look at human civilization as a single atomic structure, the negative polarity is telling us it's the end time and the positive polarity is telling us it's the beginning of something wonderful. All the basic binaries by which we lived for millennia seem to be fractured. We can't even agree anymore on what is right and wrong and what is good and bad. We have one polarity of the argument telling us that religious fundamentalists in the United States are a borderline terrorist organization. The religious fundamentalists are telling us that the people calling them terrorists are possessed by demons. Forget about a middle ground. It doesn't exist. Snaking through these two polarities of right and wrong, science and dogma, and good and evil are the most heinous of rumors that just won't go away. We're being told that millions of children are disappearing every year into sex slavery, and things even darker than sex slavery. We are being told that powerful people who are alleged to run the world are involved in dark cults that worship dark entities in competition with our creator. There's really no defense to this claim except the mainstream media occasionally being forced to write about crazy conspiracy theories like PizzaGate. And just when you think you can throw it away as paranoid religious fantasy, it pops its head up again like an endless game of whack-a-mole. Is there really a global religious cult using children for sex magic and ritual sacrifice to a god unnamed in our time?

If this is really going on at the scale that the messengers of this doom are suggesting, then why don't we all know victims of it by six degrees of separation? The concept comes from a fantastic 1993 breakout film for Will Smith, *Six Degrees of Separation*, with great supporting roles by Donald Sutherland and Stockard Channing. The premise is that the entire world is connected by six degrees of separation, where a single degree might be a friend and then another friend and then another friend. You get the idea. Take, for example, the COVID-19 mRNA vaccine. We know that the side effects of myocarditis and heart attacks and strokes are real because the media can't suppress it. There are so many celebrities and professional athletes dying that everybody knows of somebody who has died, and if the celebrities weren't enough, then everybody knows through six degrees of separation somebody who has passed away or become quite ill. I have a friend who developed heart palpitations in his early thirties. It's impossible to hide what's going on. Are there really enough unattended children in the world to allow for all this Satanic ritual abuse we're hearing about largely through Christian circles? Or are they trying to get us to convert to their religion by convincing us Satanism is real? A simple variation on the old hell and damnation tactic that kept the Vatican coffers full all through the Middle Ages and right up until today.

What I can tell you in this short introduction is that the world is a much different place than we are led to believe through our public conversations, directed by media and television and cinema and all the things that form our social consciousness. It's a world vastly different with many machinations and many layers, and it's operating multidimensionally with many people playing roles that are related to the abduction of children and ritual magic, and what we can loosely call Satanism, even if you don't believe in the Christian paradigm. It is real. But it has more to do with the Buddhist sin, which is a lack of awareness. Most of the operations of this world are carried out by regular people doing what they're told to do. They have every reason to believe what they're doing is in the public good because their superiors have told them so, and were run through institutions. What my story is going to do is examine my life and my family and my upbringing, and connect all the things going on in the world, and demonstrate to you that it is unconsciousness that is perpetuating the conspiracy, and that if there is in fact an agent that we could call the devil, then his principal job is to keep us stupid and one-dimensional, and in that regard he's doing his job fantastically in the early part of the twenty-first century, despite all the seemingly magical things going on in science.

Part II

The Devil & Us

Chapter 4

The Devil

To understand anything that you're going to be told in this book you first have to understand the devil. Everybody thinks they understand the devil. Or at the very least, they have a concept of the devil, the same way they have a concept of god. But in almost all instances they're wrong. Everything you've been told is a complete crock of shit. They don't want you to know anything. The angels never fell. That's a bunch of nonsense. What kind of a god would create a universe and have his initial creations rebel against him? If that's the level of incompetence we're dealing with in our creator then we may as well stop trying. How can we get anything right if he can't? Who would make up such a thing?

The devil of our popular imagination is the devil who made up the story about the devil. They don't see themselves as doing anything wrong. You have to see it from their perspective. To them we're another order of being. To them we're something to be played with. To them we're things that need to be told lies. And the truth would be far more shocking than any description of a so-called devil. So they lie to us. You may think you're better than that but you're not. What do you tell a child when it asks a question the answer to which is beyond their age? You tell them a lie. You understand that the developing psyche can't handle the truth, so you obfuscate. No harm in that, right? It's actually the right thing to do when you think about it. In fact it's a general rule that carries right through all of life. There's a class of human beings, the majority actually, who want to hear the lies their whole life. They can't accept the truth; they can't even conceive of a truth. And so culturally they buy what they're sold. You'd be amazed what people will believe if you put a human being in a funny costume and give them a title. I know. It's complicated. How could our imagination make something up that scares us? If our imaginations created it then why are we afraid of it? The fight or flight mechanism in human beings is only geared toward things that are real. And what's this inward fear? It's the fear of the unknown. Who am I? How long do I have? What happens to me after it's all over? You can figure out almost everything you need to know about a human being by how they answer those three questions.

If we're going to talk about a devil as a being, as an individual consciousness, then we have to go to the plural. The devil is many. The devil is most. The truth is the devil is a field of energy. That energy is the lie, the comfort of that lie, and the comfort of all the lies we tell. It's gotten so bad it's almost all a lie now. We live in it from birth till death.

I want you to imagine the most frightening thing you can. Nothing, right? You can't imagine it? Why? Because it's like putting your hand over a flame. You can't do it. You think you can, but you can't. There was a fellow who was part of that crew that got pinched for the Watergate Complex breakin back in 1972, G. Gordon Liddy. He was at a party one time and he held his hand over a lit candle. People could see and smell his flesh burning. They asked, what's the trick? He said, *not minding*. Liddy was on this personal empowerment trip, mind over matter, Nietzsche and the super man, shit like that. That's the devil, too.

The real devil is a divine being. It can be no other way. He works with the law. Like all higher order beings, the devil is best understood as energy. It's very difficult to fit him into a body, to make him like us, to anthropomorphize him. This is part of the *infantilization* of human beings. Everything gets anthropomorphized. Even god has been anthropomorphized. The energy of the devil contains the law. It is the law. The law of the devil represents the frequency that resonates with all things in this dimension, and by dimension, I mean the world, and by world, I mean the world we live in right now. The world in which you are holding this book and reading it, the world in which your mother and father live, the world in which your son and daughter live. This physical world. The world with the *New York Times* and *The Washington Post*. This is the devil's jurisdiction. This is the world that has his signature on everything. His is the dominant frequency in this world.

The devil is not a violator. He never breaks the law. That means every time you find the devil in your life, you invited him in. Think clearly and you will see all the times you invited the devil. It's also part of the system and the law — you can ask for this information. The devil is responsible for this disclosure. If he fails upon request, all contracts affected by the disclosure are presumed void. It's a lawful system. We've always had law. The only time we lose it is when we take it over. Man is subject to the law. There's very little interpretation in the law. Interpretation of the law is more for courts and lawyers and television and movies. In the real law there's very little interpretation.

There was no fall from heaven. There was no rebellion. The devil has always been here and will always be here. It's a feature of this reality. We tell ourselves these stories to understand things, but they just end up confusing things. The devil doesn't break any law. He is not above the law. We understand from this observation that the devil is not corrupt. He is the perfect example of the law. We accept the invitation for power and control over institutions and people. We become bound to the law of the devil when we want part of the devil's power, which is control over everything in this dimension.

The law is intended to maintain the peace, because peace is the agreed upon commonality of the human experience. When the law comes into effect, you will often hear an internal voice, or what we might call internal chatter. That's the devil. He's built right into us. He has a say on what we feel, what we experience, and what we remember. He's an equitable partner. You hear other opinions but they're just ignorant. Some will tell you the devil is evil. I say no. He has a job to do, and it must be respected.

I watched my mother and father talk to walls my whole life. They spoke aloud when they were alone. I suppose it's therapeutic, if therapy has any say. It's the habit of haunted people. My house was terribly haunted. All of those people at AA meetings, and all of those people at the hospital where my mother worked, they were all haunted. Walk through an asylum some time and you'll see people talking to the walls. When you spend a lot of time with haunted people you become haunted yourself, unless you have discovered suitable spiritual defense.

The law is simple. If you play with the energy you entrap yourself in a myriad of chattering invitations. The moment you listen to the chatter it gets louder. Once the chattering becomes a chorus, the power of the devil is all about you and all through you. All of the invitations given to you will be invitations into darkness. The dark is very seductive. Everybody wants to go into the dark. It's irresistible. The further you go into the darkness the darker you become. It's subtle at first. You don't even notice it, but it becomes more distinct, and then one day without knowing when it started, the chatter has turned into a conversation. Now the devil speaks to you. Do you know why? Because you've gone so far into the darkness you can't find your way out. The first thing the devil does is blind you. That way you can't go anywhere without holding his hand. And once you take his hand then the chatter turns to a conversation. Then you realize what's going on, but it's too late. If you keep going into the darkness from this point, you'll self-destruct. You activate the death wish within us. We all have it. It's built into the body, a destroyer of sorts, our own personal Shiva. The moment god invented time; destruction had to follow. Time is a lie. It always has been. The only concept of time we have is from our physical bodies. They fall down after time. They have destruction built into them. They are impermanent. We occupy these bodies. We are permanent. We are eternal. The devil wants to take you eternally into darkness. He can't really do that — you do it to yourself. The whole thing is an elaborate trick. Everywhere you go in this world you go by your consent. You inform on yourself.

Lucifer is the firstborn of god and the Morning Star, and he never left god. The fractured relationship is pure gossip. The jurisdiction of Lucifer is mind. The first concept of self we have is through thought. On the sixth day we named everything. This individuation by species and personality and genus is all the jurisdiction of darkness, the domain of the devil, of Lucifer, in cooperation with god. The thought *franchise* was passed on to man. But that doesn't mean that the devil ever gave up the enterprise. God is being. The devil is thinking — the chatter in your head. It's like a cosmic game. The goal is to capture the soul. The devil needs the souls to run the world.

Nobody gets out of here without befriending the devil. That's why the story of *the fall* is complete nonsense. You don't confront the devil. He's not your enemy. You become aware of him. You enter into a meaningful dialogue. He is respectful and polite. All he ever did was offer entrance into a room and you willingly entered. Inside that room you found your identity. You named yourself, just like the animals got named on the sixth day. And the moment you did that, you entered into a contract with the devil. It's that simple.

This is how the devil works. He offers us a choice then waits for an answer. It's not a hard sell. We can go off and think about it. Our choice determines our action. The devil does not make us do anything. He lives by law and his purpose is that of a gatekeeper, but not the gates of hell, more like the gates of experience. The devil doesn't judge. He's a test. We see it in Christ's experience of the forty days in the desert, and we see it when Buddha conquered Mara. The negative principality has many names. No society has left him unnamed, no matter how primitive or advanced — Loki, Crow, Lucifer, Mara, Satan, Shaytan, and so many more. Why would every society name a being that nobody has proof of meeting? Do you think it's some kind of collective consciousness experience? Do you think Satan is part of a pre-coded genetic disposition, the surfacing of our deepest unconscious fear? Seems unlikely we'd come up with such a defined hierarchy, whether it be the Hindu deities and demons or the underworld of King Solomon. There's a point way out there where you must be able to discern and ask yourself, what are they really talking about?

In our mythos in the West, we have an eternal struggle between a sensitive god, a god who lives and feels, and an absolute destroyer. Nothing really in between. This realm is a sincerity factory. We have to develop sincerity. Absent sincerity, nothing good can take root. Sincerity is the sun and rain of the inner world. Nothing grows without it. Unfortunately, we have become very insincere people. You can't get anywhere good without sincerity. You have to know yourself. The devil keeps you in a play, in a game of half measures until you sincerely get tired of that game.

As you play with the devil's promptings, your returns are in half measure, requiring you to double down like in Las Vegas Black Jack, to get what you should have had the first time. As you double down, the devil continues to guide the process through offering choices. Your choices either take you deeper into darkness, or bring you out of it. The devil refines you through a process of offering poor choices and this allows for laws to come into play. He is a master of the law. The devil is law. His very spirit is the law in action. Nobody calls upon law more than the devil. He loves the letters. It's such a pretty language, law that is pretty in its letters, but poison in its spirit. The devil lives by law allocated to him, from god the father of all life, and the devil is doing god's work. A delegation from god to Lucifer. The devil is law, and the law is energy.

Energies have their own laws, and higher energies supersede lower energies. This devilish energy is just that, an energy that can be toyed with by the gods, and physical beings like humans and others, and even higher dimensional beings. He keeps the insincere where they are, otherwise, heaven would be impure. All energies have laws and intelligence to them. Since this field of energy we call the devil is here on earth, it can also reside inside us, around us and in things.

The devil's color is red, the same color as the root chakra or sexual anchoring of the human body. Biology is the domain of the devil. Sex is the number one temptation given to us. Our root chakra gets lit up with an energy from outside of us. This energy can be from another person or from an energy or entity that can energize the root chakra. Dreams are infiltrated with people we know or knew. Sex is the invitation to the game. What we ignore about sex could fill a sports stadium. Sex moves everything now — crypto, cars, lifestyles, clothes, even medicine, and it does it in such a way we can't even remember when it didn't.

The pictures in our heads can come from many places. We can make the case that there is imagination based on biology. When a young boy goes through puberty he is going to have more and more images of the female form in his imagination, the place where pictures come into his head. Not only that, when he sees these pictures externalized in magazines or on the Internet, then they will immediately have a tremendous gravitas. This is because he's gone through puberty and is now sexually awakened. Not only is he sexually awakened, he is at the height of sexuality for a male. The male sexual peak is from fourteen to eighteen. So the imagination is going to be dominated by women. Makes sense, right? If you don't eat for three days because you're fasting you'll find that the image of food in your imagination is crystal clear. Suddenly imagination is more effective than it was when you were eating three meals a day and snacking in-between. You can hold the image of a hamburger and fries in your mind so clearly you can practically smell it. This is biology contributing to the imagination.

What can we deduce from this? First and foremost, biology uses the imagination, or *hijacks* the imagination might be the better way of saying it. From this we can understand that the imagination is not above the fundamentals of what we are. We are a biological entity in our physicality. Our bodies come from this earth. We have the seven orifices above the neck like the mammalian class to which we are a part. Our imagination, which is much more acute than any other animal in nature, is not above the fundamentals of what we are. It's part of these fundamentals. Or a better way of saying this is that it can be used by these fundamentals. The imagination never quite seems to be ours. It comes with tremendous force and autonomy when there's a biological necessity. When we have a creative necessity, and we try to deliberately use our imagination it seems to run away. The human brain influences our imaginative potential. Neuroscientists suggest that the imagination is controlled by the prefrontal cortex. The brain also has something called the default mode network, and it's believed to play a role in spontaneous thoughts, daydreaming, and imaginative thinking.

The default mode network has been observed to become active in brain research when tasks necessitate the creation of mental imagery or the contemplation of alternative outcomes. And then there's the internal pharmacy, the compendium of drugs the body produces to motivate. Dopamine is one that has been in the news quite a bit. It's been suggested by many people that the abuse and exploitation of dopamine discharges is the basis of social media addictions, like Facebook and Instagram and Snapchat. Dopamine is associated with rewards and is known as the *feel good* neurotransmitter. It's also been linked to creative thinking in the generation of novel ideas. It's been proven that dopamine levels influence imaginative thinking and problem solving. Serotonin is another naturally occurring drug within our brains and bodies.

Evolutionary psychologists would have us believe that the imagination evolved for higher adaptation. Our ability to envisage alternative scenarios and future outcomes allowed us a significant advantage in survival and adaptation. Our brains probably evolved — according to these evolutionary psychologists — as a means to solve problems and navigate the immediate landscape, and plan for the future. These very same evolutionary psychologists would have us believe that our narrative myths were the product of imagination for the formation of culture; Just a means of sharing beliefs, creating community, facilitating communication, and passing knowledge generationally.

Try to remember sexual stimulation in your body. What happens? Where does it begin? How does it come about? Usually it's stimulated. In the human being, arousal usually occurs visually. Although, throughout history there have been many forms of sexual stimulation. I wouldn't want to marginalize the French and their advancement in the perfume industry. So we can say that the olfactory sense is a sexual stimulant as well. But, I think if we're being fair, we can say that the largest stimulant of human sexuality is sight. Advertising agents certainly understand this. By associating any number of products with sexual stimulation they correlate sexual impulse and purchasing. In any sane society it would be psychological abuse, which would be medical malpractice, because psychology is part of the *Hippocratic Oath*, but in our wonderfully imbalanced Western society this is just business as usual. Oh sure, there were cries of outrage along the way. There were the fear mongers at the side of the road holding up their signs every decade since the *flappers* in the 1920s, saying the world was coming to an end.

Whores have always been around. Prostitution was probably the first real human industry. They go right through the formation of the United States. Every town had a whorehouse. It was actually legal for quite a while. It was made illegal in 1910 with the *White-Slave Traffic Act*. It wasn't until the 1980s that the formal academic study of prostitution in the United States commenced. It was probably a result of the AIDS disease in the gay community. The study began because there were concerns about women being forced into prostitution, sexually transmitted diseases, sex trafficking, and sexualized violence. As well it came to be understood — although it's hard to believe it was never misunderstood — that there was a connection between substance abuse, drug addiction, alcoholism, mental health, and sex work. It's not so much that prostitution was made illegal in 1910, rather it was just that moving women from one state to another for the purposes of prostitution was illegal.

It was pretty easy to laugh off the people who advocated for sexual restraint in society — nut jobs, fanatics, religious zealots — they've been the fodder of the left and the liberal media for decades. It's just reached a pitch now. Except it isn't so funny anymore. It's almost like open warfare now. What changed? Nothing. The people at the side of the road, the zealots, were right all along. It was just a slow, multigenerational burn. Aside from being invisible to human eyes, the things which live in darkness also work at a pace at which seeing them operate is impossible, or seeing their effects in one generation is difficult. It's more of a cumulative effect, but when it arrives we cannot believe what we've co-created with the things which live in darkness.

Sex in the advertising industry started slow and got racier and racier every decade. In the early seventies the pornography industry began in the United States. Linda Lovelace was one of the first stars. That's her stage name of course. She starred in a movie called *Deep Throat.* I'll let you figure out what it's about. The seventies were all about enjoying ourselves. The puritanical decades that preceded us and the tight wound nature of our grandparents and great-grandparents just wasn't going to wash anymore in the age of television, rock music and recreational narcotics like cannabis, cocaine and LSD.

Pornography has always been associated with the liberation of women among the people who profit from it. In fact they don't like the word pornography. They prefer to call it *eroticism.* It takes the physical act of lovemaking and reduces it to two dimensions on a moving picture screen. Nothing has had more effect on culture and society in the last several generations. The traffickers always found a way to make this seem consensual. According to Linda Lovelace it was not consensual. Here's what she said in 1986 — *When you see the movie Deep Throat, you're watching me being raped. It is a crime that the movie is still showing; there was a gun to my head the entire time.*

It's no coincidence that pornography originated in the society with the greatest middle class in the history of civilizations. That's not to say that America in the seventies invented decadence. Every society that achieved any measure of opulence perfected decadence. The Ottomans mastered it. The Romans absolutely mastered it. The Greeks were no strangers to it. It's just that it had never been spread across such a large swath of people before, and that was because there had never been a middle class before. There had never been hundreds of millions of people in a single society with the disposable income and the leisure time to indulge desires that had been left dormant due to the intensity of surviving and raising a family in the past. It was like we all became Roman senators.

Power is the greatest desire of men, because from power all other desires can be met, but from humility they all must be earned. It's the oldest contract in the world. Power is an illusion of epic proportion. It's the moving carrot the human mule follows. But the utter simplicity can't be ignored. I get more money, I feel better. Wake up the next day and follow that carrot all day. It's probably the most common prayer in the world. Follow the carrot. A prayer is a complete atonement. People like the simplicity of it. Follow the carrot. What happens when you get the carrot? Nobody ever gets the carrot. You were yoked and pumping a well all day. That's how we get the water to the castle. Ultimate power is the ultimate illusion — a bottomless black pit — and the self that asked for that power is the first thing consumed by it. The Faustean bargain revealed. All the devil does is open doors. You have to walk through. He's not a violator. He's a facilitator, a kind of a life coach for souls who crave experience. He's the *experience* guy. The devil can age you a thousand years in a weekend. He has that power. He loans it for interest. The devil is a part of everything that manifests here now. The god part came out of nature. The devil will come out of man. Humanity is the womb of the devil. It's a spiritual birth, a frontier broken in our minds, and it will all seem natural and good.

We are all sparks from the one soul. Our spark goes all over the universe and even other universes. The game is endless. The earth moved through a celestial time within which this galaxy has been placed, in a spectrum of low frequencies. This is where darkness, the devil, and many other things exist.

This is the blood sacrifice. It is for defilement not forgiveness of sins. Atonement is spiritual. Blood is physical. Before Christianity it was just the darkness. And the darkness is god's bodega. He puts all his tools there. Our real path is light and dark. Neither one makes sense without the other. The place we come to atop these two paths is agnostic to both. There's a strange correlation between the advancement of consciousness and psychosis. As the intertwined light and darkness braid the rope by which we climb out of the pit, so too does it demand detachment. We gain a greater understanding of the necessity of evil. Everything would break down without it. Darkness is the grout that bricks our reality together.

Our game as humans is to recover the perspective of soul. The simple prayer of greater good, remembered and applied to all decisions, is the way out. But you have to be sincere. A half hearted person has never broken free of the grip of darkness. You have to master the higher good prayer. Every decision you make must be for the higher good of all involved. There can be no exception. The process converts your own darkness into light. You then realize what all mystics do, that god placed all his secrets in the dark. Make your peace with it and celebrate the wisdom you have gained.

Everything we do, decide, and act upon lives in confederacy. We live in confederacy with unseen beings. Your decisions and actions determine the type of confederacy you have. Nobody is alone. That happens later, much later when you start to rise up. Realize that all the voices you've ever heard in your head are part of your confederacy. You might recall a parent, or a teacher you admired, but that's just a psychic sheath. You don't know what you're really communicating with. The only way you can be sure is to do everything for the higher good, and when in doubt let the shortfall, if there is to be one, fall on you. I know this sounds antithetical to the *capitalize and conquer* economy in which we are raised, but when you change your definition of profit in life you change everything. The only profit in a human life, from the perspective of the designer of human life and the various orders of angelic and demonic who administer these lives, is the perspective of soul returning, but it's not traded on the Shanghai Stock Exchange, London, New York, or Sydney. It's not traded. It's the higher economy. The irony of our time is we have never been more efficient, and never more advanced, and never more productive than we are now, but the vast majority of people live a quiet despair, unable to forecast by any means, and beset by worry and a plague of bad thoughts. It's all natural, or it was when the hurricane shook up Kansas, but now it always happens in climate-controlled environments, man-made systems and industries, cities and suburbs. So, if the storms are not real then what causes the chaos?

This devil energy, it's everywhere here, inside us, our culture, and our environment. It infects anything that comes here. It's a quantum energy, invisible and omnipresent. You can't escape it. His debts are recorded right into the fabric of this reality, and a carbon copy is made in the world above us, for safekeeping. The debts can be called, extended, refinanced, and paid, but never forgotten. The devil fulfills wishes that god ignores. He's a mirror of sorts, a cheque cashing service, payday loans, that sort of thing. Not paying your debt in the agreed upon manner increases the presence of darkness in your life. It is the providence of the lender in this situation. Everything has been done by consent. What part of the contract did your heart not understand? Did you not understand you would never hear thunder again, or see the magnificent lightning? You see it and hear it but not the same way a person free of darkness does. The notes are changed before they touch your heart. I told you, he's a part of everything here. It all exists by his grace. And you're not going to get anywhere without that simple tribute. So don't tell me you don't worship the devil. You're just too obstinate to acknowledge it.

Then, because this is a contemporary text, we have to talk about the new evil. These are what we call inter-dimensionals. They look like us. They do everything we do, but they are not hooked up in the spiritual sense. They are empty vessels, imagined best as us if we never created God, never even knew the hope of eternity for a moment, of purpose beyond flesh. That's them. They come into this dimension having taken over a small frequency range of ours. They are outside our causal field. They assume no liability for their actions. Their only job is to compel humans to do what they do. They get into bodies, into the nervous system, then they can speak right to head office, pardon the pun. I don't know how long they've been coming to earth, but they run things now. They're agents of chaos.

Irony is one of the most misunderstood things in our human experience. It's a harbinger of sorts. It announces the coming of absurdity. It's not so much where the literal and the expressed are in opposition to each other, but more a kind of cosmic fulcrum by which a mechanism in our reality is leveraged. It has to do with the conscious and the unconscious mind. It has to do with what our real intent is as opposed to our stated intent. It's an informant of sorts, something in the organization of your consciousness that informs on you.

There is a grand division between nature and man. Man sits atop nature. This is a commonly held belief in religious scriptures all over the world, and it's correct by natural law. Although you could suggest bias, all scripture is written by men, so why not place ourselves at the top of nature? It's true within the creational pattern that man is an order of magnitude beyond everything else in nature. We have a self-awareness that no other animal seems to possess. We have the ability to communicate through verbal utterances and the organization of sound, and we've codified these sounds into symbols we call letters, and we write it all down in a written language. There are still many tribes on the planet who don't have a written language. I live with one here in Costa Rica, the Cabcare. All understanding and meaning is passed verbally. Any written language they have is symbolic or idiomatic.

What does it mean to sit atop nature? It means that for the most part, nothing preys upon us. There are animals that we've had to contend with as we expanded into wild areas. There are stories about the grizzly bear hunters along the west coast all the way up into British Columbia during the gold rush. Special teams of men had to be hired to hunt the grizzly bears because of their aggression and habitual attacks on human beings. We still hear stories about the occasional shark attack or attack by bees or some other predator, but they are rare. Animals leave us alone because we mystify and frighten them. There's something unique about a human being on this planet. We are of this nature. We can see the same evolutionary patterns in the mammalian life forms that we see in ourselves. We can see above the neck two nostrils, two eyes, a mouth and two ears, commonly referred to in the Taoist teachings as the seven orifices above the neck. According to the Taoists, this represents an *order* within creation — the aforementioned grizzly bear, wolves, weasels, mountain lions, you get the idea.

We are at the top of this seven orifice mammal class, and we are separate in that we stand straight up. We stand on our feet. No other mammal on the planet is able to do this. It's unique to us. A gorilla can walk like a man for short distances, but it generally drops down to its knuckles and its feet, like all the other mammals in the seven orifice class. Everything else has a horizontal spine, where horizontal means in direction to the sun. Our spine stands straight up like a tree stock. We are reaching for the sun just like a plant.

Nature is occupied by an endless cycle of predation. Everything is preyed upon and everything preys upon something else. Insects derive most of their nutrition from inside the insect kingdom. They also eat from plant life. We see this in the leaf cutter ant colonies, and we see it in the pollinating insects. Reptiles prey upon smaller reptiles and mammals consumable by them, field mice and rats, things like this. Frogs subsist on the insect world. Spiders do a hefty job in keeping the insect world in check. When we come up to the larger mammals we see wolves attacking caribou and eating rabbits and in the more northern climates they can subsist on small ground rodents like rats and moles and mice. The one common thing in all of this is that nothing in creation derives its energy from outside the natural world. Every manifestation of life is a temporary allotment, and in many instances only to sustain the life of something higher up the food chain. We can call this the law of economy.

If we conceive of nature as a single entity, we see that it's self-regulating, self-governing, and always in balance. The various insects and animals and plants that accentuate nature are like cells in the body of nature as a whole, and their job is to perform a function and then fall away, just as a human body discards cells every seven years. Through the lens of malignant sentiment, nature can seem brutal, but the ugliness is the malignant sentiment, which only occurs in us, the bipedal mammal. We live in a time where childless urbanites will spend thousands of dollars for care and operations for a pet, all the while eating meat and never once considering a pig or a cow is more intelligent and sensitive than their condo dog, which never gets to be a dog. Nature is perfect.

We know that nature is perfect because it never lies. It always tells the truth. If the natural world beneath humanity operates as an endless cycle of predation, what does that suggest about our own nature as humans? Why would we be set atop this predation, untouched by it? Everyone has heard the expression the law of the jungle, which I just aptly explained through predation and the natural balancing that nature has at its disposal. It's like one whole thing that always stays in balance. If any one species becomes too dominant then they will run out of food and begin to starve and the balance will be restored. There are very few things in nature that can be thrown away. There was a remarkable study done on Yellowstone National Park and the reintroduction of wolves. Biologists were able to show that the entire ecosystem benefited by the return of the wolves, including the river. It was an extraordinary insight into the ecosystem of one national park in the United States that demonstrated that nature operates with the precision of a highly crafted watch, not losing a second of time over the life of a wind up. The only thing that can be taken away from nature without any real consequence to the system is us. Human beings are not needed by the natural system. We're an adjunct. We sit on top of nature and nothing in nature preys upon us and nature can do without us. The absence of man would not affect the functioning of nature and its balance or continuity in any way, and we'd take the devil with us, because he exists nowhere except within our adoration.

The human being is not free from the world of predation. It's just that all of our predation takes place within us. It takes place within the spiritual realm. The predators we have to worry about are spiritual beings and principalities commissioned with our destruction. The human world and the human game is infinitely more dangerous than the animal world and its simple model of predation for consumption. In the end it's all a game, though, but until you figure that out it's terrifying. That's why everything a human being does is shrouded in fear, and where our enemies are not necessarily rooted in the natural system, they are absolutely rooted in the supernatural system.

Darkness itself is responsible for nothing except its own existence. It pretty much keeps to itself. We don't understand what light is and we don't understand what darkness is, and we certainly don't understand the co-creation and coexistence of the two. Light and darkness are the original siblings of creation, two brothers that emerged after the process of creation began. One can't exist without the other. Everything comes paired. It's just the way this world works. To say that this is not a binary world is to not live in this world. Sure, when you get into the architecture and the physics of it, the binary law may fall away. The binary law falls away in quantum computing, but I don't think people are going to like the answers that come from going into the darkness of quantum computing. No matter where *we* go, *we* should always lead. If the experiential unit we call a human perception cannot go there first, we should not go there. I understand that math can take us there, but math is a conceptual proxy that goes into the darkness and doesn't come back. The only reason we know it still exists, is it occasionally sends messages back, and we get all excited, like we're prisoners in a solitary cell and after a long time of being alone we hear tapping and scratching on the other side of the wall that sounds rhythmic enough to be an ordered communication.

The dark was our first major limitation. It shut down everything we did. We slept at night and worked and moved during the day. Cast your imagination to a time when no man-made light existed, a time when the only circle of light you could have after the sun disappeared was a fire and imagine the courage it took to leave that circle of firelight in the middle of the night. The moon would have become our constant companion as well. Everyone would have known the cycles of the moon just as they know bus and train schedules today. A full moon might allow you to travel at night. You'd know when that full moon was coming. The moon would become a symbol and a living representative of a deity. All of these simple truths exist deep within us, but they're no longer correlated to the night and the day, rather knowledge and ignorance. There is an epidemic of ignorance on the planet. It's like human perception has been compartmentalized. It's become a node in a large human system. You are what you do. And what you do is not what you want to do. It's what you have to do to make the currency, to stay in the current of the modern world, which, coincidentally, is still a lunar system because we pay our bills monthly.

You know the old adage that absence makes the heart grow fonder? Take a moment to imagine the absence of darkness. Imagine what it would be like to live in constant light. We wouldn't even know what light is. We wouldn't even need a reason to define it. We'd have no name for it. We'd have no appreciation of it. Imagine all the things that darkness gives us. Darkness is the mother of curiosity. Who hasn't laid on their back on a summer night while camping and looked up at the vast expanse of stars speckled across the darkness and wondered what that darkness is. See if you can remember doing that. See if you can remember the feelings that you had. Was it not those two rarefied emotions of wonder and awe? Are not wonder and awe the first cousins of curiosity? Is curiosity not one of the great movers of human beings, one of the few passive and benign motivations for investigation that we have? If you study the circumstance closely, most human motivation to examine something is fear. I'll take curiosity over fear any day. This is not to say that there is no fear in the darkness, but I don't want to get ahead of myself. We'll save the fear for later.

Light is birthed by darkness, so we can say that darkness is the mother of light. The stars speckle the darkness. Every star in the sky had a beginning, and darkness was waiting for it, to hold it like a mother, to suspend it in space, to frame it as the majestic thing that it is. Darkness speaks light. It celebrates light. It nurtures and sustains light. It gives light all of its meaning.

What is true here — this blue marble in space we call home — is true everywhere. It's part of the way the whole thing has been set up. Now, don't get me wrong, I'm not talking about temporary truths. I'm not talking about the truth of temporal things. I'm talking about the truth of eternal things. There's nothing hidden from us. The law prevents it. Man was created to apprehend the law. These are not laws that are written down. The moment the law has to be written down, your society is lost. It means the connection with the heart is lost. The heart is the connection with the law. We weren't created to study the law, we were created to be the law. When the law is lost you're living in a dark age, but there we go again, maligning darkness. Do you see how insidious that is? Let me rephrase. This happens in ages where the inner light of knowledge is lost within us as a species, but remember everything that's been said — there's nothing random here. We go through these ages and periods because they're part of the cycles down here. The devil isn't making us do it.

We are fascinated with the darkness. Darkness is the greatest relationship that human beings have. We're admonished not to look at the darkness. The challenge lies in the fact that in our current reality, all the information is hidden in the darkness. It's just sitting there as a fact. If we came into creation do you not think it was to study creation? If not to study creation then why? Were we given this heightened consciousness above nature to torture ourselves? Everything you've been told is a lie. Don't confuse what I'm saying with worship of evil or inhuman actions or radical self-interest or anything else associated falsely with the darkness. I'm saying the exact opposite. I'm telling you that the path to god himself is through the darkness. In fact I'll go even further. Darkness is a form of light in the same way that ice and vapor are forms of water. The darkness is illuminated by human contact with it. But if you falter even for a second you will be consumed by the darkness. This is the ultimate test of faith. This is the ultimate test of the internal light of human beings. The internal light of god in a human consciousness is the only thing that can take you through the darkness.

Light and dark have formed the motion that creates all time and all events and all history and everything that will ever be in the present framework of reality. If light is the birth of life then darkness is the placenta that it lived within until it was born. No placenta and no life. Darkness is equally responsible for everything that is created. Darkness is the womb of creation. Light is born out of darkness. Conventional human understanding states that darkness is not an entity in and of itself but simply the absence of light. Can you imagine that? We can build a quantum computer and we can build a super collider but we can't get the basics of light and dark right. Darkness is in fact an entity. It can speak. It has a language. It can host life. It's a form of consciousness. It has its own consciousness. It has its own purpose in creation. It's a created thing. It's not the absence of creation, but for we human beings it's still the superstitious repository of all our ignorance.

Darkness is half of our reality as human beings. It's half of the creation for us on earth. Think about it for a moment. The planet we live on and the planet we were born on is half light and half dark. It's split right down the middle. If that isn't the perfect indication of a binary system I don't know what is. If you go to the North Pole or the South Pole you'll find six months of dark and six months of light. If you go down and live at the equator, as I do, you'll find that there are twelve hours of light and twelve hours of dark every day for all twelve months of the year. It's the most regular environment on the planet and probably the most balanced and hospitable for human life. So it's no exaggeration to say that for us human beings darkness is half of our life. Do you really think a creator would fabricate an existence for us as a sentient being on this planet only to be occupied half the time? If we existed midway between the moon and the earth in a space station, darkness would be the vast majority of our existence except for the dim light cast by the earth below and the moon above, but down here on the earth everything is half light and half dark. This book is the thesis of darkness.

Chapter 5

Our Last Free Breath

The last time there was anything even approximating a spiritual movement in the United States of America was in the time just preceding the Industrial Revolution and including the American Civil War. In literary circles they call it the transcendentalist movement, or American transcendentalism. It might have been, in part, a response to the Civil War and the horrors of it. Some might throw Walt Whitman into the transcendentalist movement, although he was a bit early. Whitman is famous for his epic and operatic 1855 poem, *Leaves of Grass*, which heralded in the United States a culture to reckon with, a new culture separate from Europe and capable of producing its own music and its own poetry and its own ethos, though at that time in America most of the culture had been violence.

> Have you reckoned a thousand acres much? Have you reckoned the earth much?
>
> Have you practiced so long to learn to read?
>
> Have you felt so proud to get at the meaning of poems?

> Stop this day and night with me and you shall possess the origin of all poems,
>
> You shall possess the good of the earth and sun (there are millions of suns left,)
>
> You shall no longer take things at second or third hand, nor look through the eyes of the dead, nor feed on the specters in books,

Of the major voices of the American transcendentalist movement, the one that resonates with me the most is Henry David Thoreau. Most people know him from a book called *Walden*. It's the story of Thoreau leaving society behind, and society was not nearly as developed as it is now. He goes to live in a small shack in the woods beside a pond named Walden. The book details Thoreau's dissatisfaction with society and his spiritual connection with nature. Here is the quote for which he is most known.

> The mass of men lead lives of quiet desperation. What is called resignation is confirmed desperation. From the desperate city you go into the desperate country, and have to console yourself with the bravery of minks and muskrats. A stereotyped but unconscious despair is concealed even under what are called the games and amusements of mankind. There is no play in them, for this comes after work. But it is a characteristic of wisdom not to do desperate things.

The time in American history leading up to the transcendentalist movement in the mid-nineteenth century was one gripped with blood and conflict. Men behave a certain way in the absence of enforced law. The law was stretched thin in the formation of the United States of America. It lacked the institutional stability of Europe. But it was precisely that lack of law that allowed for the individual spirit to express itself so freely because the law they fled from was a corrupt law, and a corrupt law is worse than no law.

The integration between the natives and the Europeans did not go well for the natives nor did it go well at times for the settlers. People do not give up their land easily. As we go as a people — everywhere we go — we take with us the shadow of the apocalypse given to us by somebody else's prophets, never once realizing that in the unconscious shadow of that apocalypse, we became the apocalypse for so many other people. I concede the points made in *Blood Meridian* by Cormac McCarthy, that the natives were not entirely a peaceful and pastoral people. I know from sitting in on clan meetings with the Mohawk nation in Canada that they went through a time of great turbulence about seven-hundred years ago, a time which ended only with the emergence of a great spiritual figure called the *Peacemaker*. It was the Peacemaker who brought about the Iroquois Confederacy and the first form of democracy the world had ever known. It was the Peacemaker who ended generations of intertribal warfare that had descended into rape and cannibalism. The natives of North and South America lived by a different law other than the English common law or the French civil law or the Spanish common law. There were no Jews or Catholics in the Americas and therefore the concept of law was foreign. But law is never foreign. Everything is law if you are watching closely. The sun rising and setting is a law. The rains are a law. The coming and going of generations is a law. The medicines that come from the plants are a law. The lore and the mythos within which the people lived is a law. People are never without law because law forms environment.

By the time of the transcendentalists, America had already conceded itself to the European powers it sought to escape. The War of 1812 consolidated European banking in the United States of America. And where the banks are, the law is. Of course, this is no kind of law that anybody wants in a civilized society. The banks and compound interest are part of an old law that we were supposed to let go of millennia ago. This is Babylonian law. It's been carried forward throughout human history by several dark groups. Its sole purpose is the ownership and control and eventual destruction and enslavement of societies. It never fails as long as its law is not broken. When people figure out the ruse, they rebel, but by that time, the architects of the banking system already have a military force in place to enforce their law. Almost every war in the last four-hundred years has been a war instigated by bankers. Clearly, we know that banks are not the only reason for war because the concept of war precedes banking.

I call the American transcendentalist movement the last breath of America, or at least the last breath of a free America. What happened next was the Industrial Revolution. The world's first factory appeared in the United Kingdom. They were also the first to break free of the Vatican control with the Church of England and the Bank of England. With the inception of this bank and the utility of fiat notes, Britain promulgated the British Empire, the navy and expanded their market. After one of the greatest naval victories in military history against the Spanish Armada, which represented the Vatican forces in Europe, England commenced the colonization of new lands with only the slightest of competition from the French in Canada and significant competition from the Spanish in Central and

South America. This gave us the empire which stood until the end of the second World War, after which it was decimated and power was transferred to Washington and Wall Street, where it had been gathering power in isolation from the ravages of war which had decimated Europe. This is how historians look upon it. But history is not a multidimensional science. It doesn't understand causality, magic, karma, and it certainly doesn't acknowledge the secret societies in operation. The real power in the West was held between the Vatican, London City, and Washington, and this power was represented by three artifacts of their shared religion, the obelisks, which had been brought over from Egypt — the war obelisk in Washington, the money obelisk in London City, and the harvest obelisk in Vatican City — all three of them brought brick by brick across the waters to be erected in these power centers. The failing of history is the failing of us.

The laws of our societies in the West are the laws of war. To the victor go the spoils. It doesn't seem like war, but it is. It's spiritual warfare. It is now and always has been spiritual warfare which determines the kind of society in which we live. To the vast majority of people this war is unseen. To the religiously literate it is a battle for souls. Unfortunately for them religious literacy is spiritual illiteracy. In our case the victors were the secret societies, and the secret societies have always controlled the religions in the West. The goal of the secret societies is the suppression of spiritual consciousness. If the spiritual consciousness of the population elevated to a sufficient degree, the machinations of these secret societies would be revealed.

One of the things that I bought myself when I built the earthbag house in the Talamanca mountains of Southern Costa Rica was time. It doesn't really exist, but while you're here in a body it's best to operate as though time is a precious commodity. The society I left in Canada kept everybody busy paying their bills. It had become a slave society. I hated it. In Costa Rica I elevated my spiritual practice to four hours a day when time permitted, which was between intermittent work contracts as a technical writer, the trade in which I had made my living since my son was born, mainly in the software and telecommunications sector. Remote work was difficult to find until 2021, then everything changed. Suddenly remote working was all the fashion. The pandemic had changed the norm. What was bad for others became good for me. I was able to select work and get paid a fair price.

Since I established my residency in Costa Rica, where my building's location exempts me from mortgage payments and property taxes, I am not subject to the monthly bill cycle that often leads to distress and hardship in Toronto. My water comes from a mountain stream and requires no filtering whatsoever. My garbage is largely organic and consumed by my twenty cats and two American Staffordshire Terriers, and what inorganic garbage remains is burned. Where I live, everyone either digs a septic tank or defecates in the jungle, so there's no need for sewage. There is one small school in my small mountain village. The student numbers are so low that all the grades are mixed together in one class. This was the way my mother was schooled in Westmeath, Ontario.

My whole life I had wanted to be a writer of literary fiction. Like all the others of my archetype who had preceded me, I was deeply moved by my literary antecedents —sufficiently moved to want to dedicate my life to writing. My success in the field had been small. I published one literary novel in Canada. I was reviewed across the country and all the major daily newspapers. My reviews were excellent. However, the world was finished with serious literature. The only literary market that seemed to be making its balance sheet was young adult fiction. My commitment to literature had always been vocational, not commercial. I tried a couple more manuscripts but nothing worked out for me. I thought they were well written stories, however, the literary world wasn't seeking anything resembling the content of my writing. I have never been a starving artist. Between bouts of creative writing I worked at contracts as a technical writer. I did not have a lot of savings the way people who worked continuously might, but I was all right with that sacrifice. Between meditation and creative writing and work, I had found my perfect balance. It's just that it was non-sustainable in an aggressive commercial entity like Toronto. This was the genesis of my idea to move out of Canada, this and the spiritual forewarning I had been given in my meditations about a dire future for North America.

After two years on the mountain and settling in with my wife, I started to look for things to do. I had more free time than I had ever had before. The only nonfiction book I had attempted was a true-crime book, which I had written about a gentleman wrongfully committed for murder in Canada. It was a book that came to me through a friend. This friend had introduced me to John Edmonds of Stardust Ranch. John had a story to tell. I started the book in 2012 while in Canada, but I couldn't get past one-hundred pages. I quit. It was the only manuscript I had ever quit. I don't like to talk too much about why. The material unnerved me. It was one of those freaky ranch stories like Skinwalker. But there I was seven years later with this book back in my imagination. It didn't go away. I called John, and we decided to finish the manuscript together.

John passed away in 2022. He was psychically attacked on the ranch. The main aorta in his heart, the one the doctors call the *widowmaker*, was torn in seven places. He lived another year but finally succumbed in the midst of the COVID pandemic. I mention this book, *Stardust Ranch: The Incredible True Story*, because the realizations arrived at in this manuscript would not have been possible had I not crossed paths with John and written that book with him. John was not just an experiencer of extraterrestrial phenomenon, not just the steward of a couple of time-space portals on his property, rather a man who had come to rare wisdom. There is a chapter in that book in which John and I describe the effects of the Industrial Revolution.

Basically, the Industrial Revolution is the expression of three technologies continually worked on and advanced. One is illumination at night. This is the electrification of cities and the light bulb. The second is rapid transport. This is the manufacture of the combustion engine and the ability to move faster than horse or bicycle as an individual. The coal powered train existed, but the track lines were not sufficient to get everybody everywhere they wanted to go. And the third thing was the dislocated voice which first manifested as the radio. Around this time the telephone came into common usage. These three things, electrical illumination, rapid transportation, and the dislocated voice utterly transformed us.

The Industrial Revolution did far more than that. It changed the way we think. It changed the way we perceive reality. We went from a largely rural people to a largely urban people. We went from a people who went to bed shortly after sunset and woke shortly before sunrise, to a people who were up twenty-four hours. We were bombarded with change. In no period of recorded history did the process of invention and manifestation happen more quickly than in the Industrial Revolution and the ensuing decades leading to our present moment. It happened at an alarmingly exponential rate. We went from the outhouse to high speed internet and electromagnetic railways in four generations. The two millennia preceding this leap forward saw very little change. We cooked on fire. We rode horses. We farmed, and we developed a series of useful trades — tailoring, dress making, and baking.

In truth, it did not all happen just in the last century. Very little of it would have been possible without the enlightenment, without Gutenberg's printing press, without Martin Luther taking a stand against the Vatican, and without the freeing up of thought and behavior from the strictures of the Vatican. This also freed up the Jews, who had been checked by the Vatican and not allowed to hold professional standing or public office. It had also kept their religion in check. The Jewish religion and the Jewish people are bent upon controlling the world. This is not anti-Semitism, it is fact. It is the stated fact of the rabbis, and it is the stated fact of influential and moneyed Jews around the world. Whether the Jews are destined to control the world per the edict of a god largely defined by them is something I do not care to comment upon.

I would also point out that the various forms of leadership we've had in the gentile world have been less than favorable. If rabbinical leadership and Noahide law could truly bring world peace and prosperity then I welcome it. But I seriously doubt that it could. The Jewish religion, aside from the public face we get in cinema and television, is a system of ceremonial magic. It is the basis of all the secret societies that proliferated in Europe after the enlightenment. The Freemasons, the Martinists, the Rosicrucians, the Order of the

Golden Dawn — which counted both the Irish poet, William Butler Yeats, and the Scottish black magician and demonology aficionado, Aleister Crowley in its ranks and countless others — would not exist without the Jews strategically sharing the Kabbalah. The demonic hierarchy and control thereof given to King Solomon, whether Solomon and the first temple actually existed or are just symbolic placeholders for an understanding.

I will give you the understanding I have acquired after studying numerous religions. Religions are formed in phases or cycles. A religion begins with a cycle of teachers. Taoism has eight major figures between 500 BCE and 200 AD. Sikhism had ten masters, more or less, in sequence. The theological system we call the Abrahamic system has twenty-eight major prophets. This statement may spark disagreement among some readers. Debate is a lively part of the Abrahamic system. Let's just say that our number of prophets, for the sake of the case I'm making, is twenty-eight. Of those twenty-eight, the last two formed new systems of religious practice that comprise three billion people. They are of course Jesus and Muhammad. The relatively few numbers of Jews, somewhere under forty million — with some figures being as low as fifteen million alive today — retains the balance of the teachings with twenty-six of the major prophets.

These three systems have a murderous intent toward each other at the level of scripture. There is no brotherly love in this system. They are all absolutist, not centered on reincarnation, and the most punitive of the world's religions. The Jews must discredit both Christianity and Islam or otherwise accept the prophets into the canon, which they have not done. The Christians reject Muhammad at an institutional level as a false prophet, and, except for American evangelicals who are Christian Zionists, the Jews are regarded as Christ regarded the Sadducees and Pharisees. Whether this is the true theological feeling of the Vatican and the ancillary Christian religions is debatable. Remember, in the West religion is a great business. Nobody wants to lose customers. The Islamists believe Muhammad was the last prophet in the Abrahamic system, and therefore the only prophet to be studied and followed in the time in which we now live. All preceding prophets are the linguistic calculus that validates Muhammad's position. All who disagree are fundamentally infidels to be put to the sword.

The religion that we have been given in the West is bad religion. Good religion does not contradict itself over the course of three phases of history and geography. Truth is universal, not regional. This inability to reconcile our spiritual identity and create a clear path back to the divine, so that each generation can produce masters, is why the West never became civilized. I can't say what happened to us. I can stumble about and theorize. I could say that there is such a weakness for power in the men of the West that god gave up on us. In actuality, god never gives up on the people. God is nothing if not a persistent force. The more apt way of describing it is that we gave up on the idea of true service to god. We turned god into a weapon. We turned god into a social construct. But perhaps the one thing we did above all else that nullified god's ability to communicate with us, is we institutionalized him. God requires no institutionalization.

I do not believe that god rejects hierarchies or assigned roles and purposes to individual beings, both the corporal and spiritual, but I am quite sure that he never creates institutions. The deformity was sown right into the roots of the original prophets in the original scriptures. The moment that god said that he had a chosen people he was a racist. God no more has a chosen people than he has a chosen plant. When you come to understand what god really is you realize that his love for a tree and a human being is the same. The only difference is the human being has a higher degree of awareness of that love if he or she so chooses to exercise that franchise. It's that simple. God is a persistent force that animates all life in all dimensions and in all universes and timelines. The rest is what we make of it.

One religion above all others sets itself apart in the West. This is the religion of negativity. This is what we could call Satanism. Although, based on my understanding of Satan and the demonic legions, Satan himself would be as disgusted with his living adherents and the people who use his name as Christ would be when he comes back and sees how his name is used. Satanism has its roots in a few different religions, but it mainly comes from certain sects of Judaism.

All you have to do is open your eyes and look around you. All those gods that were supposed to be abandoned by the Jews at the edict of the one true god, those horrible gods from the ancient days of captivity in Babylon and Assyria and Egypt, those are the gods in charge now. This was the dark side of the enlightenment and Gutenberg's printing press and the Geneva Bible and the King James Bible and Protestantism. Please don't infer from my statement that the Vatican was any better. It wasn't. It had succumbed to the abuse of power centuries beforehand, if it ever had any legitimacy to begin with. The Vatican created the cardinal sin of institutionalizing Christ. This is perhaps the greatest sin of the last two millennia. Interestingly, the Catholics omitted it in their catechism. So much for authority. There is no protagonist here. If you thought I was going to say that the Jews are worse than the Romans or vice versa you're wrong. They're all bad.

The Industrial Revolution changed everything. And what did we do with this newfound time through illumination at night and newfound productivity through manufacturing capacity? We upped our war game. War has always led us, at least in the West. It is truly the great game of our human race. We're not happy unless something is dying. After all, something has to be punished, otherwise why did god give us all these rules? We live in a world run by child rapists and Satanists who tell us that we have to kill for god. If that isn't the very definition of irony I don't know what is. The first world war was devastating. War has always been fought on front lines, but never had a front line been so entrenched before. The war was literally fought in trenches. This was largely due to the capacity of firearms at that time. The machine gun had been invented. Why invent something you don't want to use? Boys died in unheard numbers compared to previous wars. After all there's only so many limbs that can be hacked off with a sword or an ax before you get tired. Not so with belt fed guns. They called it *the war to end all wars*. Then we had another one twenty years later. We super sized it. It was even more spectacular in its carnage than the first world war. Go big or go home. It was in the Second World War that we invented the weapon that would stifle war, the big bombs. The world ending bombs. So then we just scaled war down to military police actions, which means we bullied the shit out of smaller countries, all the while frowning upon bullying in our domestic culture, a classic do as I say not as I do scenario.

In the West we have been conditioned to do as we are told. It's not just the West. All people are conditioned to do as they're told. The difference in our culture is there's no back door. In other cultures if you want to go and explore the universe you can go and study with professionals. There are numerous systems of consciousness development in India and even in the Chinese satellite countries like Taiwan where most of the Taoist and Buddhist master lineages settled after the Cultural Revolution. In almost every culture outside the grip of the Abrahamic system, god has been an exploration that can be undertaken and realized in a single lifetime. In our ham-fisted prophetic system we are told by our betters, who are allegedly the agents of god, that we can never be that, and to just follow the instructions from god. It's the most spiritually pathetic system in the world. The only reason it has persisted this long is the material benefit. If we hadn't hooked into the Industrial Revolution and the age of invention, our society would be a laughingstock. We are fundamentally an uncivilized people.

Our material prosperity is due in large part to the direction of the secret societies, the practitioners of ceremonial magic. This is the real religion in the West. Most of it springs off the Kabbalah. The secret societies proliferated about four-hundred years ago. It's a long and complex story that could be its own manuscript, but, briefly, what happened is the Vatican lost its grip. There was an opening in the power chain and it was seized upon. It was largely the work of Germans. They got it started with Jakob Böhme, the myth of Protestant mysticism, the Geneva Bible, and the printing press. It's a mistake to think that this has anything to do with European populations outside of the Jewish diasporas.

The Jews had a long and colorful history of expulsion from European nations. They claim anti-Semitism. The public records claim abusive money lending, sexual perversion, and human sacrifice rituals which have come to be known as blood libel. These were the secret societies before they proliferated into the Protestant world. It's debatable whether the Jews wanted to share their Kabbalah magical technology with gentiles, but a strategic decision had to be made, either share it or go back under the power of the Vatican, who were well aware of what the Jews were capable of with their magical systems if left unchecked.

The Vatican itself was hacked with the crypto Jew Ignatius of Loyola. He founded the Jesuit order. The Vatican already had its own magical system which had been incorporated from another nefarious group that we can loosely call the Black Nobility. They are a network of families that source themselves all the way back to antiquity. Some might even suggest they possess the Atlantean technologies and the Atlantean consciousness.

To understand the mentality of these secret societies and their adjunct of science in its present expression, you have to understand what it is that they value. They value knowledge and manifestation. In a sense they are the Luciferian consciousness. If we strip away all the childish notions given to us by the Bible and the ministers and priests who have enforced it for two millennia, we can see clearly that Lucifer is pure mind. The Western secrets societies are a kind of perverse yoga in which the result of the yoga is not manifested within the individual practitioner but externalized in the form of a technology or ritual. Whereas yoga in the East, as given by Shiva in Vedic tradition, is for the transformation of the individual into light and knowledge. The Western systems are for the manifestation of this knowledge. They are involved in power, plain and simple. And what greater power could there be than the power of manifestation?

It's not that other societies are stupider than us, it's that they had more respect for the basic design. We have always been about sacrilege. The enlightenment has been a desecration of the whole. The idea of honoring creation and the human life and its cradle of nature is repugnant to us in the West. If the human race is infected with a virus then we are the ones who carried it.

For the unwashed masses who are not elected to enter into the secret societies, we are left to the edicts of our prophetic betters, *do as we say, these are the edicts of god and as proof we give you knowledge of the future.* Here's the problem with that. Time is malleable and dependent upon what the individual human beings alive during the time cycle manifest in their thoughts and feelings. If a document is put in front of them in a formal manner, a ritual manner for that matter, given to them by a robed priestcraft who themselves are an elect few capable of reading the spoken word, then that's going to have quite an effect on people.

The individual thought processes contribute to the prophetic edicts as a kind of self-fulfilling prophecy. There is no future but what we make and if we're all contributing to the making of a future prophesied then the probability of that prophesied future coming true is highly likely. The individual consciousness is harvested by the ritual. The illiterate peasant and serf is an unconscious co-creator in a magical ritual.

The proliferation in education hasn't changed the status of the illiterate peasant that much. The quality of a high school education or even an undergraduate degree in the present system is so abysmal and misdirecting that it may as well leave you at the same state as the illiterate peasant or serf. But a peasant is not burdened with the arrogance of a misguided education, and it is indeed arrogance, because modern education denies god. Please do not confuse my words with the rambling of the faithful. It is not my intent to convert you to the dogma of any faith. However, the belief that we are absent the guidance of a loving overall intelligence is the greatest ignorance in the West. Here's the irony. It is a deliberate ignorance fostered by those who know better. It is the intent of those who worship the negative principalities to have us believe that the overall chief doesn't exist. The steward can only rule the kingdom in the absence of the king.

The only reason human beings exist is for spiritual realization. We were not created for material advancement. That is an entrenched illusion that the darkness has brought about, the product of the Industrial Revolution, and a number of theories that are completely nonsensical, chief among them being the theory of evolution. The very nature of consciousness is such that it's able to alter the physical environment. We see this most acutely in what religion calls a miracle, but miracles are shunned because they compel people to believe something by a force. The law of free will demands that all people who come to spiritual life do so because they have arrived at it naturally and without any force. This is why no religious institution can compel you to believe or practice and why the devil and his minions can't simply take over human beings at will.

Evolution is the adaptation of the body to an environment. It's a passive and slow miracle that is allowed. When people migrate due to calamity they may end up in an environment their body has not lived in for many generations. They may go from a subtropical environment to a very cold environment. Over a number of generations the body of the people who live in the cold will adapt. Physiological changes will happen in the body and will be born into the children.

This is the truth about evolution. It's the relationship between consciousness and reality. Everything that exists is consciousness in some form. A rock is consciousness in the form of a rock. A human being is consciousness in the form of a human being. If everything is consciousness then it stands to reason that adaptability to the environment is a natural process. Darkness has hijacked the theory of evolution and despiritualized it to suggest that ultimately it will be okay for one group of people to kill another group of people, because it's really just the law of natural selection in operation, and if nature does it, why can't human beings do it if we're the aggregation of all natural law? You see how subtle that is? That's the way the darkness works. It gives you a percentage of truth and then mixes it with a lie. It's not really the darkness that we can blame. Both darkness and light require agency to express themselves. It's a human being who becomes an agent of the darkness or it's a human being who becomes an agent of the light. The forces themselves cannot express without agency. This is the truce between light and darkness. They have to form rules and they have to work together. In this reality nothing wholly positive can exist and nothing wholly negative can exist. There has to be a ratio of the two at all times.

Materialism has radically transformed the way we think. This is what the sages and the mystics were warning us about. It wasn't really about greed. That's just the cover story. For something to be true it has to be eternal. That means it's true in all conditions and times. We want to believe now that there's a big difference between the past and the present. We want to believe that we've advanced tremendously. We have advanced materially and regressed spiritually. That's the way it all works. Everything has to stay in balance. That's the way light and dark work and that's the way everything else in this binary system works. To think it's any other way is to invite catastrophe.

Let's take sex and gender as an example. We want to believe in the modern age that there's no difference between men and women. A man can do what a woman does and a woman can do what a man does. If that's being a clerk in an office then yes. If that means the ability to buy a condominium and make the mortgage payments then yes. It's true for the condition in which we live now. However, the condition in which we live now is not a permanent condition. We've already hit resource limitations that are suggesting a depopulation as a solution to the problem by the elites. If you haven't picked up on that you're just not paying attention, or it's just too dark for you to contemplate. However, it has already been clarified earlier that darkness is half of reality. You're missing at least half of the picture if you don't contemplate darkness. So why don't you contemplate darkness? Because you've been taught that it's evil. Maybe you read some horseshit self-help book that told you positive thinking is the way to guide your life. Excessive thinking, over-thinking, it's all negative. Why do you think all the lineage schools advocate meditation? Where do you think expressions like chatter of the mind came from? Thinking is necessary for us to cope with and survive in this world but an overt reliance on thought as the resolution to all problems is the cornerstone of our materialistic religions and philosophies in the West, and they go well with prescription antidepressants.

There's nothing evil about darkness. Evil is the instruction through our religions that darkness is evil. Are men and women equal? Of course they're not. If we were the same thing, god would have created one thing and one thing only, and we would pull children out of the ground like carrots. In this system for anything to work the positive and the negative must combine. A man and a woman must combine to make a child. Certainly we're very close to, or we've probably even surpassed the point where we can create children out of nothing and they haven't released that information to the public yet, but for the sake of this text let's just assume that you still need a man and a woman to create a child. I won't say which is the negative and which is the positive because I don't think there is a universal definition, let's just agree that they're the two elements of a binary system that are required to create life. Men and women can both be positive and negative depending on the function or the role they're fulfilling in the natural system. In the natural system men and women are not the same. The strength of the male is required to physically build a house and to do all of the work necessary to support children. There's absolutely nothing chauvinistic about this. Convincing people that this is chauvinistic is evil. Every human civilization from tribal to complex has arrived at the same conclusions. Men go into the world and get what is needed for the home to continue and women generally stay at the home or close to the home with the children. There have been no exceptions to this rule. The material world has been a grand exception to this rule.

Chapter 6

1947

The year 1947 was rather extraordinary, a crossroad in the timeline of humanity, a redirection, the commencement of a public narrative that would enforce what they started in the Industrial Revolution, the nail in the coffin of human consciousness, and the insurance policy that a free breath would not be taken. It's really always been about consciousness. Once you see it, you cannot unsee it.

If your understanding of the Second World War is from conventional history, then you are completely and utterly ignorant of what really happened. It's not your fault. The narrative dominance they established when they illuminated cities, created dislocated voice technology like radio, telephone, and cinema, and the automobiles and rapid transportation was intoxicating. Who would question that? Nobody. The only reason it returns to the fore of consciousness now, in the early twenty-first century, is that the Fourth Industrial Revolution is so blatantly Satanic, so devoid of spirit and beauty, and such a full commitment to darkness that it's natural to go back to where it all started — the farm to the city, the late eighteen hundreds — because, as I have already said, once you see it, you cannot unsee it.

Not many people have had the courage to articulate the tremendous symmetry, the uncanny similarity between the Nazis and the Zionists. It would be difficult to come up with a better billing in the world of professional wrestling — ladies and gentlemen, in this corner we give you *god's chosen people*, reviled and vilified by Christendom as the drinkers of children's blood, the blood libel cult that has terrorized villages and hamlets for centuries, stolen gentile children, and worshiped dark entities, and in this corner we give *the master race*, blond haired and blue eyed, ravaged by a war not one generation past, savaged by the exploitative and unreasonable Treaty of Versailles, and now back for a rematch, more cunning, more diabolical, and fully versed in the occult and off-world technologies of the demonic Jew. You can't make this up. I dare you to even try.

In terms of sheer inventiveness and productivity the Germans were unmatched. They broke the Vatican through Martin Luther and Protestantism, which curiously, did not endear them to the Jews for eternity, as the Vatican had been a stalwart oppressor of Jewish liberty in Europe, where the vast majority of Jews resided. Like the Jews, the Germans had a racial identity under the Nazis that was otherworldly, supernatural, and exceptional. They openly spoke about eugenics and cleansing the earth of the racially impure. It's no secret that the Jews are equally hermetic in their racial superiority, but, where the Germans were open and direct in their rhetoric and beliefs, the Jews preferred the backroom, low fanfare of commercial control and usury through banking and money, a world in which they had gained a considerable foothold with the war for the British throne in the sixteen hundreds — Cromwell, the Stewarts, William the Orange, and the Amsterdam Jews (Sabbateans no less, apostate Jews) who wanted the central bank charter for what would become The Bank of England — and, some might argue, it was these very Jews who made sure the Germans had the screws put to them in The Treaty of Versailles, which, according to most rational observers, was the inevitable catalyst for the rise of Hitler with the promise to release the German people from the perpetuity of squalor, exploitation, and endless and irreconcilable debt, the Jewish hell.

Curiously, the only thing even approximating the Nazi racial hegemony in our time is Noahide Law, now being openly advocated by many rabbis in Israel and in the diaspora, a system of living in which Jews are openly acknowledged as being superior, and, within which, they will rule from Jerusalem. The master race and the chosen people should both be equally reviled, but, alas, it's not the case. Protestantism snakes its way back to Judaica, — its intended trajectory all along — as certain to the Hebrews who assisted the Biblical translations of both the Geneva and the King James Bibles as the migratory path of Canadian Geese in winter. The Protestant movement went right back to the root, cutting out the Latin speaking middleman in the Vatican. We find more and more support among the clueless Christian Zionists for the Jewish supremacy which should have died a public death as certain as the master race. But wait, it gets better. The Nazis were not really defeated either. Yeah, sorry to be the bearer of bad news, but the Second World War never really ended. The Nazis were never defeated. Nuremberg was a theater. The decades-long hunt for alleged Nazis by Simon Wiesenthal and his like, is an extension of the theater. The real Nazis are alive and well, preserved by the otherworldly alliances they made during the war and the human confederacy they created, which, having taken a page from the Jewish book of low key operations, remains clandestine, but you would be surprised by the offices and titles with which the undying Nazis collaborate.

One of the things that the Nazis became involved in was mind control. Mind control has become epidemic now. It began with a simple technique called *psychic driving*. This was repetitive stimuli upon the mind. It took many forms. The subject would be blindfolded and earphones would be placed on their head. Classical music might be played from one side, and the other side would blare something more noxious, more like noise than music. The Nazis had figured out that the left and right sides of the brain were almost like separate entities, segregated from one another like blacks and whites in the American south around the same time. Through the manipulation of the mind, alternate personalities could be created, fragmented selves which could come and go, and each had no knowledge of the others, no memory of the others. This was an absolute and cardinal rule of the alters, so much so that if one of the alters murdered five people and the police apprehended the afflicted person, the interviewed alter being would baffle the police and pass a polygraph test, and why? Because the alter really had no knowledge of what the other personality had done. It gets weirder than that, though. Most of the literature on this topic stayed within the fractured mind and alternate personality thesis, but I believe it's more spiritual. I believe that the alters are disincarnate spirits, and, in some instances, in the later developments of the program, which has not died and lives on to this day, demons. My basis for this thesis is a friendship I made with a seventh-generation super soldier, that included two visits on his part, to my mountain home in Costa Rica. Both visits were interrupted by his handlers because of the natural healing properties of the place I live, the Talamanca mountains in southern Costa Rica, which are quite possibly the most biodiverse thousand square kilometers in the world, and, as a statement of fact, are a heritage site under the United Nations Environmental, Scientific, and Cultural Organization (UNESCO).

This goes back to the point I tried to make in the opening chapter of this middle section of the book, *Last Free Breath*, which is that everything is scientific, psychological, and not related to the spirit and the larger human being, the parts associated with but outside of the body. Curiously, both the Zionist and Nazi factions maintain this code of silence to this day, as do many of the commentators coming into the topic sideways, most notably American Christians who have wandered into it only to assure us like rabid parrots that it's all demonic. The problem with that thesis is, they don't really understand what demons are. Not many people do. Most people who claim to have an understanding of them are religious and just parroting their scriptures, coupled with the experience of one or more exorcisms.

Remember, the fulcrum of the deception is the misalignment of context and detail. Demons are actually a very natural part of the human exosystem, fire elementals for the most part, and then there are other things more daunting, but it's not worth detailing them because their impact on human beings is negligible. The fallen angel story is nonsense. The Lucifer story is nonsense. Ancient Aliens is correct on most of these topics. It's all an extraterrestrial story, but the demons themselves are part of the original elementals. The job of the elementals is, as the name suggests, elemental. Demons are cleaning agents, like maggots, rats, and cockroaches, part of the class of organisms and entities we fear simply because they remind us of death, which is the mother of all fears for most human beings. Love a butterfly and hate a maggot, but the maggot does much more work than the butterfly, and in consuming dead things, hastens the decomposition of the dead mammal which might otherwise spread more disease to living organisms. Fire elementals do the same work on planes above us, immolate things which if left to linger would pose harm to the ecosystem above us — as above so below. The final similarity between the Zionists and the Nazis is they both experienced massive culls in their population. The Jews allege six million in the Holocaust, and the Germans allege eight million lost in the death camps after the war ended, which might very well be the most brutal and largely unspoken atrocity of the Second World War, but remember this; Jews are not Zionists and Germans are not Nazis.

One of the most remarkable things that happened in 1947 is the Roswell UFO crash. In my opinion, it really happened, though there have been countless official voices trying to make anyone who believed it seem stupid. This is where we connect the dots. Remember the thesis of the Industrial Revolution? It's about shock and awe, technological supremacy so swift and so overpowering that no one would doubt the official voice on anything else. This is an age of reason, ladies and gentlemen. The age of superstition is behind us. There are no such things as UFOs, or, as they're called now, Unidentified Aerial Phenomenon (UAP). The headline from the Roswell Daily Record on July 8, 1947, reads as follows: *RAAF Captures Flying Saucer on Ranch in Roswell Region*. The story was countered by the Roswell Morning Dispatch and the headline: *Army Debunks Roswell Flying Disc As World Simmers With Excitement*. The headline is passed exactly as it appeared, including the capitalized articles *As* and *With*. It was small town journalism.

Roswell has been the source of extensive speculation. There are sources out there who suggest that the Roswell crash was faked, and that it was a Satanic ritual to infect the minds of human beings. Here's what I think. The nuclear testing was like a multidimensional flare. Nuclear testing and nuclear weapons have the ability to affect not only the physical dimension but also ancillary dimensions, ones where all kinds of other life exists. Suddenly the human condition touched other beings, entities, and perhaps even individuated forms of life and expression that are neither beings nor entities. Things heretofore unimagined, not even in the unholy work of Lovecraft, things we were not prepared for, and still are not prepared for, but one thing is quite certain, these closed doors were opened by the Nazis, or, at the very least, the keys to these doors were made by the Nazis before they had the chance to open them.

If you've been paying attention to the UFO narrative in the year 2023, you would have noticed — beyond the regular public sightings of mysterious orbs of light, tic tacs and unidentified craft which perform physics-defying aerial maneuvers — that a US Congressional hearing was held on July 27th, which for the first time in America's history, saw three senior military officials, explicitly questioned about UFOs. These three officials were: David Grush, former national reconnaissance officer of the UAP Task Force Department of Defence; Retired US Navy Commander and F/A-18 pilot David Frevor; And Ryan Graves, executive director of Americans for Safe Aerospace. These gentlemen claimed that the US government was withholding and concealing information about a longstanding secret program that retrieves and reverse engineers off-world technologies.

There is a *space race* that continues well beyond the assertion that Americans landed on the moon in July of 1969. It is a global exopolitical race to develop off-world technologies, materials, zero-point energy and hybrid biologicals. The extremely questionable ignorance of governments to these Top Secret programs is largely due to the highly compartmentalized nature of the subject matter and the way in which clandestine three letter organizations and corporate military contractors like Lockheed Martin and Raytheon, withhold, and license the *Blackbox* knowledge, and keep it in their back pockets like a wildcard for future use. This technocracy, like the new mythology of the twenty-first century, is forward looking. But it's really just a smoke screen and a side story to what's really going on.

What's also interesting to note at this time in history, is that the Manson murders took place three weeks after the phony moon landing. After twenty years of research, Tom O'Neill —the Vanity Fair reporter— published a book titled *Chaos: Charles Manson, the Cia, and the Secret History of the Sixties*. The Manson murders took place on August 8th 1969. The eight and the eight are symbolic and Satanic culture. I'm not crazy here. There is an absolute correlation between black magic, the Third Temple of Solomon and that whole Satanic crowd, the Extraterrestrial movement, and space and extraterrestrials. But let's not digress.

From the wreckage of the scout alien spacecraft which crashed at Roswell New Mexico, a living pilot was recovered and sequestered within the facility we know as Area 51. A young American Army nurse by the name of Matilda MacElroy would be the only human to successfully communicate with the extraterrestrial. Matilda retained a copy of her typed interview transcripts from 1947, and nearing her death at the age of 83, forwarded them to Lawrence

Spencer, who in 2008 would publish them in a book titled *Alien Interview*. In her letter to Mr Spencer, Matilda said *The status quo of our government establishment has been to "protect the people" from knowledge of such matters. In fact, the only protection afforded by ignorance and secrecy is to hide the private agenda of those in power to enslave others.*

Much to the frustration of executive military staff at Area 51, the surviving alien chose to communicate with Matilda alone, and could only do so via telepathy, as it possessed no operational mouth, and no ears or nose. The body of the alien was a doll of sorts with large eyes. It had hands and feet with three digits that had some small ability to grasp things. The *doll body* is the most fitting analogy, as it required no food, no water and no oxygen to survive. The body was neither mechanical nor biological, though it did have an electrical nervous system similar to ours. It was animated by the energy of her spiritual being and the doll body was the most suitable device to be able to operate in the physical world.

The alien identified itself as *Airl* of the *Domain Expeditionary Force*. According to Airl, the role of the Domain Expeditionary Force is to preserve and protect the property of the Domain. Whilst on a mission to investigate what Airl called "burning clouds", radioactivity and explosions, the scout alien spacecraft was struck by atmospheric lightning, which caused the pilot to lose control of the disc. This race of extraterrestrials has intentionally refrained from contacting humans because its edicts are to observe and not interfere, but they have been to Earth several thousands of years ago and were familiar with the Sanskrit language of the Vedic Hymns. Humans of that time period would report spacecraft as Vimāna —mythological flying palaces or chariots.

By the fifteenth day, Matilda had assisted Airl to develop a stronger grasp of the English language and the core aspects of our culture and religious beliefs. The gallery of military staff and psychologists supervising and monitoring the interviews would prepare questions in advance for Matilda to present to Airl, but rather than answer direct questions, Airl chose to give specific information:

> I will provide information to you that I think will be beneficial to the well-being of the immortal spiritual beings who comprise humanity, and that will foster the survival of all the myriad life forms and the environment of Earth, as it is a part of my mission to ensure the preservation of Earth.
>
> Personally, it is my conviction that all sentient beings are immortal spiritual beings. This includes human beings. For the sake of accuracy and simplicity I will use a made-up word: "IS-BE". Because the primary nature of an immortal being is that they live in a timeless state of "is", and the only reason for their existence is that they decide to "be".

An IS-BE is immaterial and exists outside of space and time. Every IS-BE has an individuated spirit and a unique identity, power, awareness and ability. Airl says that *there are many other intelligent lifeforms in the universe.*

Airl referred to one of these lifeform races colloquially as the *Old Empire* —simply because that race of IS-BEs inhabited Earth before The Domain took control — and that this race had bases of operation in our solar system. The Old Empire employed a form of electronic screen or net. If, after the death of the body, an IS-BE attempts to penetrate the force screen, then it is subjected to an extremely high electrical shock, which results in the erasure of all its memory, including the totality of all past lives.

> The shock is intended to make it impossible for the IS-BE to remember who they are, where they came from, their knowledge or skills, their memory of the past, and ability to function as a spiritual entity. They are overwhelmed into becoming a mindless, robotic nonentity. After the shock a series of post hypnotic suggestions are used to install false memories, and a false time orientation in each IS-BE. This includes the command to "return" to the base after the body dies, so that the same kind of shock and hypnosis can be done again, and again, again -- forever.

As such, the Old Empire has essentially been using the Earth as a prison planet for potentially millions of years.

> So, when the body of the IS-BE dies they depart from the body. They are detected by the "force screen", they are captured and "ordered" by hypnotic command to "return to the light". The idea of "heaven" and the "afterlife" are part of the hypnotic suggestion -- a part of the treachery that makes the whole mechanism work.

Eventually, the Old Empire was vanquished from this solar system, but the force field technology that perpetuates this cycle of birth-death amnesia remains hidden and operational. Now that there are no attendant Old Empire forces on the planet, other extraterrestrial races have imprisoned their “untouchable” IS-BEs on earth, as if it were a galactic gulag. This may explain why there is such an unusually broad mix of races, cultures, and personality types on earth.

For any kind of galactic rescue operation to be successful, it is critical that IS-BEs on this planet remember who they are and rise above the enforced amnesia cycle under which we are held hostage. Humanity must largely develop in its own time and with little interference. The Domain is observing the "Human Experiment" and Airl states that *humanity is at a point in its history where it is approaching a period of extremely high pressure and darkness,* but that this crucible of events is required for the good in humanity to evolve.

Alien Interview may read like a grand space opera, and Lawrence Spencer clearly states that he was unable to corroborate much of the story, but it is very interesting to note the exponential increase of UFO activity after 1947, and the congruent commencement of nuclear weapon testing in New Mexico. The supplemental footnotes in the addendum of *Alien Interview* cite numerous reports, affidavits and eye witness testimonies relating to the Roswell incident.

NASA Astronaut Neil Armstrong states the aliens have a base on the dark side of the moon and that the *aliens warned them to get off and stay off the moon.* Milton Cooper, a Naval Intelligence Officer not only confirms the moon base, but that the Intelligence community named it *Luna.* Independent VHF receiving facilities, such as backyard HAM radio operators, have intercepted messages which were bypassed by the NASA broadcasting outlets stating that Apollo was directly observing spacecraft which were monitoring them.

The expansion of the American space program began in earnest after that historic journey to the moon in 1969. Public opinion soared and government funding of public money flowed into the coffers of NASA and contracted civilian business interests, which focused on jet propulsion systems and electronic technology. Humanity was enamored with space and true to Gene Roddenberry's slogan, it really seemed to become the *final frontier*. How naïve. If anything, it became a new frontier for science and technocracy. But space travel became beleaguered with failures. Rockets exploded, space shuttles disintegrated, and astronauts died. Money evaporated as quickly as the rocket fuel out of those booster rocket engines. Future spending was reinvested into the development of computing, Silicon Valley, the Internet, communication, social media, supersonic flight and new weaponry.

One thing for certain is that every space flight which humanity undertook, was not a giant leap for mankind, but a metaphoric casting of breadcrumbs which left a trail for any extraterrestrial race to follow back to our home planet. Every time we went into space, we brought something else back with us. And every nuclear weapon detonation, was a scalar beacon pulsing throughout the time and space fishpond, advertising our presence and our infantile propensity to dominate, control and kill each other.

The Oppenheimer narrative recently depicted by the brilliant Christopher Nolan in his similarly named film. Oppenheimer is pure fiction. The Nazis built the bombs that are alleged to have been dropped on Hiroshima and Nagasaki. They were secured after the German surrender. They originally had New York and Los Angeles painted on their respective sides. The US military painted over the city names.

If the theory that nuclear explosions summoned otherworldly things to our frequency of reality is true, then it stands to reason that out of self-interest they would begin to investigate by sending scout ships first, which is exactly what the ship in Roswell was.

This is not to say that extraterrestrials have not always been a part of the human experience, but in the past it had more to do with inception races and guardian races and exploitative races who had been clandestinely interacting with the human race for as long as the human race has been on this planet. This is something which would have been known only to small handfuls of people on the planet, extremely advanced souls incarnated here on spiritual missions, certain secret societies who worked with alchemical or spiritual texts from bygone times, and the generational holders of the secrets of Egypt, Babylon, Sumeria, Persia, and other antiquated societies who had openly interacted with races from other dimensions or other parts of this time and space we call our galaxy and universe.

The extraterrestrial movement has spawned a significant debate in the human race, with a contingent of people — religious leaning — who would have us believe that these *extraterrestrials* are in fact demons, practicing the demonic craft of deception for the acquisition of immortal souls. This is in some measure true. The spiritual realm can trick us, but they are not demons, per se, just non-physical tricksters amusing themselves for no more gain than that, like adolescent boys ringing doorbells and running away or lighting off firecrackers. This is a good time to quote Shakespeare, when Hamlet says to Horatio on the appearance of the ghost of Hamlet's father, to which Horatio finds himself in a cognitive dissonance — *There are more things in Heaven and Earth, Horatio, than are dreamt of in your philosophy.* All due respect to the Bible, literal and ignorant utility of its verses redacts relationship with the divine, when the purpose of spiritual practices is to increase relationship with the divine. But we cannot dismiss entirely the foray by the tin roof evangelical into the melee. There is something spiritually *fishy* about the extraterrestrial movement.

There is a very strange character to the early days of rocket science, the corollary to the fusion and fission that creates the bomb. The bomb is useless if you can't deliver it. One of the main figures in these scientific advancements was Jack Parsons. He was also a Thelemite Occultist, the system founded by Aleistar Crowley; He was also known as the *beast* and the *wickedest man in the world*. What a strange pastime for such a brilliant man. Parsons was intent on manifesting the antichrist on earth. In early atomic bomb testing he and his colleagues placed an infant inside a lead case within proximity of the bomb test site, and this was their crude formula to bring in the antichrist. Don't ask me to explain it. It's as batshit crazy as it sounds. The salient question is why are these people doing this, and, more specifically, why is there so much dark religion associated with NASA, the characters of this time, and this zeitgeist throughout World War II? Do you know who else was deep into the occult? Yeah, you guessed it, the Nazis. Hitler and his inner circle, the upper management in the SS, were steeped in ritual and magic. So, where did everybody learn all this magic?

To understand how we arrived at this chaotic mess we have to go back and correct some errors. There really is no such thing as a *Jewish* religious tradition. The tribes that associate themselves with Judaic tradition were scattered across that region of the world. Egypt was the center of what we might call mysticism, but even that isn't the correct word, because mysticism denotes a connection with god, and I'm not sure that the Egyptians had a connection with god. They were certainly a multidimensional people, and they were certainly versed in portals and magic and manifestation. This cannot be denied. This is why the Western secret societies are fascinated with Egypt. Egypt represents the last bit of consciousness associated with the age before the one we're in now, which is the Iron Age, or, as I like to call it, the *ironic age*.

The term Israel represents a conglomerate of tribes. It never really existed. There were a number of tribes that remained in the near east, mainly the Canaanites, the Assyrians, and a few others. They went to Egypt. They were not taken there as slaves. That is a historical lie. So in a period of time, the patriarch we know as Jacob, went to Egypt with his son Joseph. The Torah tells us that he was kidnapped because his brothers betrayed him. The historical reality is he married the daughter of the chief high priest of Egypt, and Joseph became the prime minister of Egypt, a high figure that led into all the esoteric teachings of the Egyptians. These teachings were basically appropriated and coded into the Torah, but coded in a way that they are almost completely inaccessible in the modern age. The Kabbalah has been able to decode a lot of it but not all of it, and so the Jews don't even understand the technology they have. That's the simple truth of it, and here we are again, 1947, just after World War II, back to the Nazis and Zionists, the two polarities of this atom from hell, both intent on splitting the atom, the Nazis succeeding, the Zionist forces — what history calls the allies — stealing it from them in the form of two prebuilt bombs and dropping them on the Japanese civilians. And the guy they gave credit for this, in a brilliant Edward Bernays style spin, was Oppenheimer, who was Jewish. You might be wondering why I'm skipping over Einstein, another Jew, and a German to boot. He is the ultimate Zionist public relations victory, and really little more than a plagiarist, fraud, and poster boy of the campaign for the *chosen people*.

Magic relates to the manipulation of time and space. It can deal with predictions, manifestation, curses, and the application of extreme psychological and psychic stress upon another human being, call it a curse or call it what you will. These things are generally done from the fourth dimension and many cultures on the planet have figured out how to do it. In polite modern society we don't talk about these things, and we've relegated them to superstition — big mistake. It was a mistake on the part of the general populace, but it was the intended outcome of the architects of the Industrial Revolution. Anybody who wants to control humanity has to first suppress the natural consciousness of humanity, which is multidimensional and able to see through many things. The suppression of consciousness is done through socialization. You teach the parents. The parents teach the children. The children teach the grandchildren, and after a certain number of generations the lie gets embedded or hard coded into the genetic line of the culture. Thought affects our DNA. This is why the key to unlocking the secrets of reality are done through meditation in the eastern systems. The *absence* of thought and the *accessing* of higher energies illuminate and reset the DNA, so that we can think and feel in different ways, and, most importantly, think and feel on more than one dimension. This is the secret of secrets. This is the hidden treasure of all the secret societies. It's all the same thing. Our Western system has been a hack and a con since day one. Whatever multidimensional consciousness we have in the West is the product of stolen Egyptian magic masquerading as Jewish mysticism.

And then there's Moses. Moses was not a Jew. He was a blood-borne Egyptian, a disciple and priest taught by the Egyptian priest craft, and this explains the great mystery of the Temple of Solomon. Its construction was as mysterious as the construction of the pyramids. More interesting is the idea that the first temple never existed, nor did Solomon, the most revered of the non-prophetic Jews, as he was not a prophet, and the inclusion of his material in some Christian religion — *The Song of Solomon*, *Proverbs*, and *Ecclesiastes* — is more a cultural window into the early Jewish state before the destruction of the temple and the captivity. Solomon is revered by Freemasons, the secret society commenced by Jews in the seventeenth century in England, culminating in the London and Scottish grand lodges in the early eighteenth century. Many accomplished contemporary black magicians, like Tim Rifat, who alleges to have been trained by the Rothschild dynasty and was last known to live in Vietnam, the result of running afoul of MI6 and the CIA, claim the real Kabbalah was never given to gentiles, and that the version given to non-Jews is ineffective and dangerous. Just like the Nazis, the Jews identify by blood and genetics.

One of the most curious things to come about from 1947 was a woman — though even that designation could be debated — by the name of Cynthia Crawford. I first came across her when I wrote *Stardust Ranch: The Incredible True Story* in 2019. My co-author and the steward of Stardust Ranch, John Edmonds, told me the story of Cynthia.

Cynthia was created in 1947 by the mixing of human and alien DNA. Her father had been a member of the Office of Strategic Services (OSS), the progenitor of the CIA. Cynthia visited John at the ranch in Arizona around 2017. She had also been living in Arizona, yet they had never met, despite both of them having exposure in the world of exopolitics. She stayed at the ranch for three days. John told me they felt related in a cosmic sense. Two days after leaving Stardust Ranch, Cynthia died. She had a brain tumor. She knew she was dying. One of the last things she wanted to do before leaving the world was visit John at Stardust Ranch.

Cynthia Crawford took a public role in the American exopolitics movement, speaking at conferences and fulfilling a step by step mission, as she described it, because her full mission was withheld from her, and this, she said, was because if she had known her full mission too early on she might have failed. What one immediately notices is the almost religious language. It's a one to one match. If she claimed she was being led by angels it would have been a prophetic mission rather than galactic, and there's the thing to note. In this year of 1947 we get the seeds of a transition or a translation, but the language itself is not changing. It's all English. The translation is from mytho-poetic language, the language of scripture, to a more literal language, from angels and demons to good and bad extraterrestrials and intradimensionals, beings who come from other places and times. Like angels and demons, the event when experienced is largely internal but there can be external phenomenon. In the Bible, angelic forces often come in dreams, or an internal, mystical experience, and so do most extraterrestrial experiences. The difference being there is no doubt about the extraterrestrial experience. The contactees know where the extraterrestrials come from, their star system and planet, the number of light years away, and, very often, they are told that they are spiritual members of the race in a contact. Abductions are another story. In the religious analogy they are more demonic. I'm not going to rehash the whole topic here. Karla Turner's *Masquerade of Angels* cannot be improved upon.

The thing which Cynthia became known for, her legacy, if you will, is sculpture. Cynthia was able to interpret the star family that an incarnate human being came from, the extraterrestrial *seed race* of which they were a member. The exopolitics narrative suggests that all human beings originated somewhere else, and are part of another galactic race, and were sent to this planet to incarnate once or many times. The service she provided was a sculpture of their race, usually a bust. It came with directions. The recipient, upon receiving the sculpture by courier, was to sleep with it for the first few nights.

Subsequent to the publishing of *Stardust Ranch: The Incredible True Story,* three people found their way to me after reading the book, three people who had received a bust at the cost of several thousand dollars. All of the stories I heard were horrible. Two were something akin to the phenomenon in a movie called *Insidious,* a successful Hollywood horror franchise focussing on demonic botherance. Both of these people had to destroy their sculptures after the first week. The third and final recipient has been a friend for several years now, and not only did he receive a sculpture, he was also a visitor to Stardust Ranch and a friend of John Edmonds. As an added bonus he was Indian by ethnicity and British by upbringing, so we shared a common language rooted in meditation and Indian spiritual concepts. He is the holder of three degrees from Oxford, one of which is a medical degree, though he no longer practices as a doctor. His experience with the sculpture was quite extraordinary. On the first night he slept with it, he woke and went to the end of the bed to have a two-hour conversation with his mother, which might not sound that extraordinary except for the fact that his mother had been dead for years. Subsequent to that he had health problems. Unlike the other two recipients of the sculptures I spoke with, he did not destroy or discard his in the first week out of sheer terror, largely due to the positive experience with his mother.

The security apparatus that evolved out of the Roswell crash was unprecedented. The extraordinary tale is documented in a book titled, *The Day After Roswell* by Philip James Corso. It was published in 1997, a full fifty years after the incident. But is it real? Remember the litmus test, for something to be true you must have accurate details and context. There is no way for anyone outside of the Roswell area or its controlling authorities to know for sure, but the details are compelling. Many people were warned not to speak about what they saw, both civilians and low ranked military. Without turning this chapter into a thesis defense on the veracity of the Roswell crash, I will concede that I believe it, though many have tried to say it did not happen, most notably the head of the US Military's Psychological Warfare Division, Colonel Michael Aquino, who, as it happens, also commenced a Satanic religious denomination within the ranks of the military. He was also a deep occultist and black magician, and he has been accused of being at the center of a child sex abuse ring at a daycare associated with the Presidio in San Francisco, a former naval intelligence office and now a public park. Aquino's story, echoed after his death by a protege by the name of Douglas Dietrich. The point to be taken as it pertains to this book is that extraterrestrials and Satanism have been entwined for a very long time, almost since the beginning of the topic, with religious fundamentalists, usually Christian, saying that extraterrestrials are demons. As you have seen for yourself by the ample data provided in this chapter, there is a lot of latitude to entertain the idea when you look at all the freaky personalities in history, like Jack Parsons and Colonel Aquino.

The Cynthia Crawford story answers a lot of questions about the extraterrestrial story we have been told, which begins with Roswell.

Cythia was created by a group within the US Government that existed above the OSS and its heir the CIA. All the named groups in the National Security Act, which was written in — yeah, you guessed it — the year 1947, have turned America and the Western world into the police state we now live within. This makes the UFO and its natural habitat, space, the fulcrum of the new narrative, the new mythology, and what is truly fascinating about this new mythology is that it looks forward, not backward. The religious mythology of the West has always been looking backward, that magical time when prophets came to the earth, more than two and a half millennia for the Jews, two thousand years for the Christians, and some fourteen hundred years for the Muslims, who have the most contemporary prophet in the Abrahamic system. This created a backward looking mythology, one rooted in the past. The extraterrestrial mythology has us looking forward, and it just grew and grew after Roswell. Gene Rodenberry wrote *Star Trek* and it became a mainstay of Western culture that has persisted to this day, with reboots of the franchise in almost every decade since it was taken out of mothballs with *Star Trek The Next Generation* in the nineties. How could they have recovered an extraterrestrial from Roswell, with the crash happening in early July, taken a DNA sample from the living alien, and created a hybrid in such a short time? Cynthia blows a giant hole in the theory of a completely fabricated UFO timeline. That's why she made her appearance in the nineties, so nobody would make the connection. Why did the invisible rulers, who some call the *deep state*, in its infancy back then, formed from the scorched earth and mass death of World War II, allow the subject — Cynthia — to announce herself? Why didn't they tell the world they made a human alien hybrid? None of it adds up. If they wanted it to be a secret, then why did they allow her to talk publicly in the nineties?

The hybridization program was run out of Edward's Air Force Base, which was linked to Philip Corso and Roswell. The four corners of the base had the north and south points connected underground to S4 and Area 51. Little is known about Cynthia's parents or family line, and that makes complete sense, as she was half alien, but the human half is most curious. If we were to give an ethnicity to Cynthia it would be German-Jewish. You can't even make this up. I dare you to even try. Crawford was her married name. Her birth surname is unknown. She had children, but they disowned her. Cynthia had one sister, a twin, and this certainly explains the Nazi experiments on twins because, if you haven't figured this out yet on your own, once you blow through the Roswell cover story as the inception of the extraterrestrial narrative in the West, it all begins with the Nazis, who were, as has already been stated, steeped not only in bizarre science like this, but also the occult, black magic, rituals, and spiritualism, mainly centered on the creation of portals. As most magic is, portals are doorways to other worlds, times, places, and spaces, even other universes, but god had his reasons for sealing domains off from each other. We are all learning the hard way now, thanks to the belligerence of Kabbalah and Nazi magicians, and the Jews being the progenitors of most of the magical traditions in Western secret societies. The Germans, having been hospitable to the Jews through Martin Luther and the Vatican takedown, were one of the first European societies to be allowed into the sacred world of the Egyptian magic that Moses pilfered. My best guess is that in typical German fashion they mastered it and perhaps even posed a threat to the Jews, kind of like when the Russians became really good at hockey and the Canadians took it personally because, hey, that's our sport.

Chapter 7

The Human Devil

One of the people I spoke to extensively when crafting this book, indeed a major inspiration for this book, was Carine Hutsebaut. In 1984, a refugee boy followed his older brother to a football game in the city which, in many ways, is now the capital of the globalist system, Brussels. The child was six years old, and he did not have the permission of his mother, but he decided to stealthily follow his nine year old big brother to the game. That was the last time anyone heard from the child.

Carine was a young mother herself at the time. She became transfixed by the story, following the news daily and feeling more helpless as the missing child's frantic and tearful parents pleaded for police assistance to find their missing son. He had vanished without a trace, and, ultimately, he would be lost, presumed dead, most likely murdered. It was a gut punch for Carine. She had a daughter the same age as the missing boy. It was easy for her to understand what the loss did to the parents, the impact it had on the parents.

She reached out to a friend on the Belgian police force. They were waiting for eyewitnesses or testimonies. For years afterwards, posters for missing children appeared on the streets and telegraph poles of Belgium. It was as though that first six year old boy in the eighties was an initiation for Carine, an initiation into a dark and terrifying world, a world which — god help her — seemed to be growing year after year, metastasizing like a cancer. Had it always been there, she wondered. Was the first child her attunement to a problem which had always existed? No, she reasoned, it was in fact getting worse, and she was right. What was once an unspeakable act of horror has grown into a new normal in the Western world, and especially Belgium, the capital of the world's globalist organizations.

Nearly forty years later, Carine sits in a plain home office in Brussels where we meet for online meetings. She has been a wealth of support on this book project. Her eyes are kind, her voice confident, but she appears tired, fatigued, drawn out as she approaches her seventh decade on the planet, nearly four of them immersed in the world of child killers. Carine is a world-renowned sex crime and pedophile profiler. She is the European version of Clarice Starling from *Silence of the Lambs*, but her expertise lies in the field of child sexual abuse, child serial killers, and child trafficking. She has been studying and working in this profession since the first missing six year old changed her life.

Carine's long list of educational qualifications include but are not limited to: The Gracewell Institute in Birmingham UK, University of Liverpool UK, FBI Internship at Quantico USA, Washington University and College of Law USA, Centre International de Sciences Criminelles – Université René Descartes Paris V, France. She has worked with numerous agencies — the Justice Department in

Brussels, Human Trafficking & Child Sex Abuse Commissioner at the International Tribunal for Natural Justice, and she is a senior faculty advisor at the NEU School of Natural Law. She speaks five languages, has written numerous books, and been interviewed countless times. She has helped rescue and rehabilitate hundreds of children and adults, and advocates for the *rehabilitation* of pedophiles.

She recalls her initial placement at the Gracewell Institute, where she was training with a group of fifteen child sex offenders. Of those fifteen, four were women. Women are more cruel than men, she concluded, an insight which runs contrary to the post-modern and perpetual victim status of women, which has now morphed into third and fourth wave feminism. She also learned early on that gender is not a limiter for child sex predation. There might be a preference, but they'll take either gender in a pinch. It's more about the destruction of innocence. Sexual predation is rarely about the act of sex at all. Molestation is about control. But why children? More often than not, the predators have themselves been abused as children, but there are sometimes exceptions. In Carine's book *Child Hunters*, she explains that sexual predators often grow up in families where they lacked parental love, emotional support, and encouragement.

There are five forms of abuse which have a high potential of producing an adult who will develop a psychopathy of child sexual abuse.

1. Emotional abuse, such as calling the child ugly or stupid, or that no one will ever love you.

2. Psychological abuse, such as locking the child away in dark places, closets, attics, basements, starving them of drink or food. A child has no sense of time like an adult does and fears that the

imposed conditions will last forever.

3. Physical abuse, such as slapping, beating, burning with cigarettes or irons, and sometimes cutting them with knives.

4. Substance abuse, such as forcing the child to consume alcohol, drugs or medications. Often, one or both parents will have an addiction. Parental relationships tend to be highly volatile and unstable. Children fear that one of the parents will be assaulted, or siblings may be assaulted, or they may be touched if the parent is intoxicated. If there are multiple children in the household, then they must take responsibility for parenting their brothers and sisters at an age at which it's significantly beyond the child's ability.

5. Sexual abuse is the most horrific and will generally mean that other forms of abuse are already present, such as the emotional and physical abuse involved in the act of rape, and the psychological impact of the act taking place in hidden locations, with threats of humiliation or death to loved ones if any secrets are revealed.

When a child suffers three out of five of these abuses, then it is highly likely that post traumatic stress disorders will develop.

There are two categories of sexual predators: the impulsive and the methodical. Christian Van Geloven falls into the latter. In 1991, on a hot autumn day in the south of France, Muriel and Ingrid, two ten-year-old little girls from the town of Elne, were out walking to buy candy. Van Geloven, a Dutchman with a recurrent pedophilic disorder, kidnapped the young cousins and took them to an apartment. There he commenced the torture and repeated rape of the ten-year-old girls. Numerous other sexual atrocities would be committed before he strangled them both to death. He then disposed of the small bodies by throwing them into a seventy-meter ravine. Van Geloven would be captured by local police ten days later after confessing the crime to a priest and allegedly attempting suicide.

An impulsive killer tends to commit sexual atrocities with the intention of shocking society, and fully intends for the bodies to be found. They are typically not educated, have poor social skills, and live with their mother or alone. In contrast, the methodical types are intelligent, well educated, and have good jobs and a family. They are nice neighbors who attend barbecues. Van Geloven was wealthy, married, and had two children. On the morning of the crime, Van Geloven had been chased out of his home village and was talking with his wife as he drove south toward the town of Elne. Carine recalls bizarre facts about the freakish marital relationship between the killer and his wife, such as his wife masturbating him in the bathroom whilst he looked at pornographic images of children being molested, which he had purchased under the counter at sex shops in the Netherlands. He had convinced his wife that it was normal.

In a cold stone prison in the east of France, Carine came face to face with the Monster of Elne, as he was suitably dubbed. She was convinced that Van Geloven had raped and killed many other children, and that it was likely that several were killed whilst he was working in the United States over a period of eighteen months. The first interview with Van Geloven went very well, and they both talked for hours. Carine describes him as a very nice and charming man. The next interview was starkly different. Carine's initial reaction upon Van Geloven being brought into the cell was shock — surely the guards had delivered the wrong prisoner. His eyes had become entirely black. His mannerisms were highly aggressive — he was a completely different man to the day before. There was no way for Carine to engage with the individual, because as she looked into its eyes, she found no connection. She forced herself to show no emotion despite the onslaught of verbal attack and intuitively felt that she was also being subjected to some form of spiritual attack. As the attack intensified, Van Geloven grabbed Carine's hand and began to squeeze it. Despite the pain, she showed no emotion and slowly brought her other hand over the top of his. The warmth and care of that touch caused Van Geloven to shake and tremble, and over several moments, she saw him return to himself. There was no other way for Carine to describe the experience, other than that of an encounter with an evil presence within a possessed man. During his rage, Van Geloven appeared to shift shape, his facial features would alter so much that he was nearly unrecognizable, and that there was an intense coldness about him. The intensity of this encounter left such an impression on Carine, that she developed a hypothesis suggesting the presence of a dark spiritual dimension influencing these criminals. In future cases, such a hypothesis seemed more feasible than what traditional psychology could adequately explain.

Carine maintained contact with Van Geloven throughout his incarceration and upon investigating his family background, she discovered a childhood that was beyond horrific. She learned that he had a sister, and that both had been heavily abused as children. As a young boy, Van Geloven would sleep in the same bed as his three-year-old sibling and witnessed her being brutally raped by friends of the family almost daily. At the age of eleven, the rape would result in pregnancy, which was subsequently solved by an abortion, conducted by the family on their kitchen table. This was such a common practice that Carine compares the events to those of a cult.

The long arm of abuse did not only touch the children within the Van Geloven family, but also young Christian's mother who was sexually mistreated and bashed. When Christian was four years old, an aunt would take him to Paris because it was fashionable to have a child as an accessory. On the streets as a toddler, he recalled that he had inclinations to destroy things of beauty and would dig his squeezed fists into the small of his back to restrain himself from carrying out the deed.

Throughout Carine's career, she has interviewed many child killers and pedophiles. Her observation is that once the offenders are engaged with compassion, eye contact and honest conversation, they become like an open book and are very willing to speak. They suddenly feel as if they exist and are validated because someone is talking with them. They see that their extremely destructive behavior is a result of being conditioned, through trauma, to block the reception and expression of love. Things of beauty serve as a universally recognized expression of love, and a killer's proclivity to destroy things of beauty is a direct and outward manifestation of their upbringing. They massacre children also because it reminds them subconsciously of their own psychological massacre.

Every human being can be metaphorically expressed as the three balls which make up a snowman. The upper sphere, representing the head, encompasses aspects related to rational thinking, intelligence, and planning. The middle ball encompasses everything associated with emotion, spirituality, love, caring and empathy. The lowest sphere pertains to sexuality. In a normal developed human, there is a smooth flow of energy between these spheres. Abnormally developed people will have highly disproportionate concentrations of energy in the lower sexual sphere, and the higher cognitive sphere. The energy is not balanced equally amongst the spheres and cannot flow freely. Hyper-sexuality and sex addiction takes root under these conditions, and offenders will often seek a sexual release from five to fifteen times a day. Sex addiction and the resultant behavior is a clear indication that the energy pathways and spheres in the snowman model are broken. The higher the depravity and perversion, the more likely it is that the energy circuits and middle spheres have been permanently destroyed. A broken circuit can be repaired, but requires significant work, and in many cases those circuits are irrevocably fried and almost always result in recidivism. Therapists who facilitate these programs are required to have intense focus and concentration. They must be vigilant of repeating patterns of body language, verbalization, tone of words, and trains of thought.

Sexual addiction has become very prevalent in Western society, largely due to the internet and the massive proliferation of free pornography. Statistically as of September 2023, pornography accounts for thirty-five percent of all internet downloads. Twenty five percent of search engine requests are pornography related. An estimated forty million Americans regularly visit porn sites and seventy percent of these are men between the ages of eighteen and twenty four, and they will visit porn sites at least once a month. There are over four million adult websites comprising twelve percent of all websites in existence. Internet pornography accounts for twenty percent of total ecommerce in the United States. Nine percent of porn users in the United States are children under twelve years old.

Habitual masturbation is an open door for psychopathy. During her training in California for the subject of psychopathy, Carine submitted a thesis to the interviewing panel, in which she intensely disagreed with the overall opinions of world specialists and therapists when they say that *the killer has no empathy.* She went on to explain that empathy is not the same as compassion. Killers are the most empathic people on the planet because they know what pain is, they know what denigration is, they know what humiliation is. They have lived through it, so they know exactly what to do when they torture and cause pain to their victims. They have no compassion because no-one had compassion for them. The entire planet did not care. Carine received one hundred percent on her exams at this university, not because she read papers and books, or scientific reports or medical journals, but because she had spent the time in front of the killers, talking with them, listening to them, observing them and seeing their personalities switch.

From a logical standpoint, a methodical killer exhibits high intelligence, making it futile to engage in a mental battle. A lot of their energy is stored in the head of the snowman model. However, the realm of emotion resides in the middle sphere, and trapped within this prison is the inner child confined since youth. Here is where true engagement occurs because Carine talks to the child in a maternal tone, *don't eat chocolate, we're going to eat in fifteen minutes. No mum, no mum, I won't. Ok then, fifteen minutes later you come back and the child has chocolate all around its mouth. Have you been eating chocolate? No mum, no really. Are you sure? Well, one little chocolate egg. Ok, I ate them all.* And it is in this manner that the child reveals all.

The *Affaires des ballets roses* was a sexual abuse scandal that was made public in France during the late 1950's. It involved twenty-three prominent men and women, political and social aristocracy, who belonged to the National Assembly. One of the attendees was the president of the National Assembly. In a luxurious country residence on the outskirts of Paris, known as the Pavillon du Butard, ballet performances with young girls between the ages of fifteen and seventeen were held, concluding in orgies. In the following legal proceedings of 1960, twenty-three individuals were found guilty and subsequently convicted of offenses against morality. The phrase Ballets Roses would become synonymous with child sex rings, as would Ballets Bleu — rose denoting pink for little girls and bleu denoting blue for little boys.

There is a dark consciousness that has a significant presence in the governing of our world. There are sinister forces and dark entities which are part of human cosmology. The ranks of elite Western society stand on the shoulders of their forebears, and no-one arrives in positions of power by chance. The foundations of Western civilization are mortared with the highly organized and ritualistic elements of secret societies and religious orders, such as the Masons and Rosicrucians. They are the extremely powerful ruling authorities and governments. They are found in banking systems and think tanks and three letter agencies. Their tentacles reach into every industry from the military industrial complex to mainstream media and entertainment. They are found in all professions: police, schoolteachers, and priests. I've cast a wide net here but please don't misunderstand that not all these types of people are involved. They are perhaps the one percent of the population who commit these acts. My point is that they come from all walks of life and are typically those you least suspect.

On the surface, sexual abuse, and indeed abuse in all its forms, is as old as time itself. The mechanism of this abuse is a transactional economy. Power and control are facets of the same stone. The perpetrator controls the victim and feeds off their fear and revulsion, and the act is sometimes consummated with a sexual conclusion.

Men soon discovered the weaknesses of other men and used these sexual weaknesses as mechanisms to gain control through bribery. On a spiritual level, the psychic energy of the trauma that is released during a child sacrifice or molestation is the food upon which dark entities will feast, and in exchange, depending on the scale of the transaction, the participant is given wealth, foreknowledge of the future, longevity, magical destruction of their enemies and anything else the imagination can contrive. In a sacrifice, the spilling of blood and the subsequent death of the victim are the greatest tokens of value in this economy. Man quickly worked out that sacrificing an animal had less value than sacrificing a child.

For Carine, the first signs of political interference and corruption around child sex abuse became obvious in courts of law around 2004 where she had to testify and defend the reports she made for criminals and victims. Of note was the Marc Dutreaux case. The testimonies heard during this trial would firmly reveal to Carine, that which she already suspected — the presence of a network whose tentacles extended to many levels of government, aristocracy, law enforcement and royalty.

Dutreaux is a convicted Belgian serial killer, rapist, and pedophile. His early crimes revolved around the abduction and rape of five young girls in 1989. After three years in prison, he was released on parole. He was arrested again in 1996 after becoming the primary suspect in several cases involving the abduction, rape, and sexual abuse of six girls aged between eight and nineteen, four of whom were murdered. He was sentenced to life imprisonment in 2004. His accomplices in these events included his wife Michelle Martin, Bernard Weinstein, Michel Lelièvre, and Michael Nihoul. All of these would receive prison sentences except for Weinstein who was murdered by Dutreaux. Dutreaux testified that Nihoul was the ringleader of their group and that he was merely a lowly ranked footman carrying out the orders of his master. Several of the statements made by Dutreaux to the police and criminal psychiatrists alleged that he was trying to hide and protect the young girls from being sent to a more sinister prostitution ring being run by Nihoul, and although he admitted responsibility for numerous sexual assaults and murders, he stated that he was not a lone wolf predator.

The implication of a broader pedophile and prostitution network would miter well with the generally complacent and incompetent investigations carried out by Belgian police. During the trial, one of the judges would resign when his close connections with Nihoul were made public. Nihoul was a well-connected businessman known to attend sex parties. Several potential witnesses around the case were murdered or died under mysterious circumstances. Some of these informants had important information about Dutroux and his accomplices. Criminal associates, witnesses, journalists and investigating police would be found dead by poisoning, car crashes, alleged suicide, shot, or beaten, choked, and dumped in a river. A letter from Judge Jean-Marc Connerotte — who was the first judge assigned to the case — to King Albert II stated:

> This institution seems to acquire its authority over sectors of the justice system by relying on a complex and secret modus operandi, that of the appropriation of certain key circuits of our institutions created and regulated by the Law. It is a matter essentially of political, financial, police, and media circuits. This mafia-style criminal phenomenon is evidently not peculiar to Belgium, but it involves particular manifestations that are well

> suited to this small country. We can imagine the obstacles that a judiciary inquiry will meet when investigating such facts: numerous taboos, problems of mentality, and a lack of cultural reference on the issue in order to be able to become aware of or deal with such criminal phenomena, taking advantage in Belgium of official reticence in terms of their acknowledgement, which favors or supports their occultation. The function of a criminal system of this sort is obviously to serve its fundamental purpose, the pursuance of particularly profitable illicit activities, such as money-laundering, and to protect the legitimacy of its activities and the impunity of its agents. This indispensable function corresponds to the motive of criminal protection that assures the permanency of the incriminated system by means of the infiltration of the certain circuits of our institutions, especially the police force, a veritable knot which my whole investigation has come up against.

The belief in a pedophile network which included high level members of the Belgian establishment fueled the public and when Judge Jean-Marc Connerotte was removed from the case, over three hundred thousand Belgians participated in what became known as the *White March* through the streets of Brussels. The public demanded a full investigation and a complete reform of the police system. In Dutreaux's *dungeon of death* where the girls were held, over six thousand hairs and pieces of DNA evidence were found that have not all been identified and accounted for. At least seven law enforcement officers were arrested on suspicion of having ties with Dutreaux. Dutreaux's own lawyer stated that *there were many devils in this case.*

The first judge, Jean-Marc Connerotte, appealed for witnesses to come forward during the early stages of the trial. These people became known as the *X Witnesses*, because they feared for their lives and wanted to remain anonymous. Carine explains that Regina Louf was given the codename *Witness X1* in the Dutroux case and she was the first one who spoke out about the networks on the highest levels. She had remained anonymous for a very long time, but ultimately came forward and testified in court. The first time that Carine interviewed Regina, she explained the mechanics of snuff movies which were filmed in a restaurant not far from Brussels. Then she mentioned names, the director of the airport and the minister of defense, who was in contact with the CIA. The system of bribing and controlling people initially used the tool of child sex abuse, rituals and parties. Les ballets rose and les ballets bleus on the highest level.

Regina Louf's family history is marred with sexual abuse from an early age. She had been prostituted out by her mother and grandmother from the age of four. Her grandmother was married to the chief commissioner of police. At the age of twelve, Regina and many other children would be forced into sex parties and orgies. Attendees at these events included Dutreaux as well as businessmen, politicians, police and justice personnel. The orgies were all filmed with the intention of using the material for blackmail and bribery. Some of the victims of this child sex ring were murdered so that they could not notify authorities. Regina's testimony would be aired on public television during the first stage of the trial under Connerotte, but the new presiding judge, Anne Thily, would dismiss Louf's statements declaring her story a fantasy as Louf had named several elite members of Belgian politics and business.

The assertion that there are many fingers in this pie is without doubt. Dutreaux owned ten houses — how did he amass such wealth as an unemployed electrician or a low ranked network footman? Why is there such a long list of deaths associated with the investigators and witnesses in this case? Because people in executive positions desperately wanted to keep it quiet. When you harm children, you disrespect the future of your own species and your own society. This is an attack on the human species. Pedophilia is a crime that even the most hardened of prison inmates and seasoned criminals find abhorrent because they understand that sexual or physical abuse against children goes against the natural cosmic order of life. This is why pedophiles are killed in prison. Most organizations formed to combat child sex trafficking are funding and facilitating it.

These networks exist throughout all of the Westernized world. I'm not picking on Europeans. Child trafficking serves many purposes within the networks: they are used as tools for blackmail, they are a source of money via child prostitution, they are used in child sacrifice rituals, they are consumed as a form of cannibalism, their organs are harvested, they can be used to control their parents, their young minds are easily susceptible to programming via mind control, they are a source of stem cells, and as we've seen in previous examples, they are a means to satisfy the sexual appetites of pedophiles. How has it become possible for our society to commodify children like this and why is it becoming more prevalent as humanity advances into this technical era?

Climbing the ladder of success and gaining access to the upper echelons of an international organization takes great sacrifice.

Brussels is a financial center of Europe, and a national and international hub for rail, road, and air traffic. It is the de facto capital of the European Union, the political and administrative center of the North Atlantic Treaty Organization (NATO). Brussels hosts offices for the International Monetary Fund (IMF) and scores of world banks. Ronald Bernard became a major player in the world of finance and turned into a whistleblower, exposing what the elite do, and who they really are. Ronald could see the flow of funds and large-scale transactions, and to see the bigger picture of where dollars were being funneled and for what purpose. There are people within the banking system who really know the truth of what is going on. With governments and multinationals, you interface with secret services and terrorist organizations — all groups involved with big money. You think that secret services are there to help the people, but they end up being the criminal organizations who finance and contrive wars between nations. Secret services also have flows of money, and they trade in drugs, weapons, and people. It happens world-wide. Finance is the backbone of this world.

Ronald's conscience was overwhelmed within the circles of the financial system. He signed confidentiality agreements never to disclose the companies, governments, or people involved. He describes the key players in the financial system as Luciferians who genuinely and reverently serve a dark spiritual entity. It's not like a Christian faith where most people are casual attendees of a church, these Luciferians are very devout and committed. At one point, Ronald was invited to participate in the sacrifices of children, but this was his breaking point and he turned his back on a life-long career and fled to the United States. He explains that these sacrificial ceremonies have been going on for thousands of years and the

Bible is full of references to these practices being carried out by the Israelites. Ronald is clear on this, *we must tackle the financial system because it is the head of the snake and the root of all misery.*

Sophie (not her real name) was kidnapped from her parents when she was very young by another family who belonged to a class of society, she calls the *Ubermensch.* The Nazis called themselves Ubermenschen. Sophie described these people as those who are gifted spiritually in the dark practices of Satanism and black magic. They carry out the sacrifice of children and adults in ritual settings. Sophie says that a significant portion of the human and child trafficking market is utilized for these sacrifices and that this is one of the world's darkest secrets. The way that this network continues to operate and remain hidden is by taking the children, blackmailing families, and manifesting their dark fantasies. The children are indoctrinated and so traumatized that they are mentally and physically scarred for life and live in fear, or become themselves possessed by demonic entities. Sophie was quite literally raised by torture.

It was common practice to have her loaned out to families who would torment and sexually abuse her and have the children of those families torture her. Her handlers would have a list of things that those families could and couldn't do because she was always so close to death. But Sophie was never allowed to die because she was such a valuable token of blackmail against royal families, organizations, and important people. This type of activity is typically referred to as a CIA Brownstone Operation, whereby the agency embroils politicians, business executives, celebrities, or anyone they wish to leverage cooperation or information from. It's one of the oldest tricks in the book. People who have unusual political power or unexplainable wealth are often found in these circles, and it's because they're usually the front men, such as Epstein and Alefantis.

From a young age of five or six years old, she was sometimes taken to places, such as mock theaters, where there were other children — typically non-Belgian refugees — and then forced to make the unbearable choice between which child should live and which must die. She vividly recollects that there were dark skinned children and that the proceedings were always filmed and made into snuff movies. The most overwhelming feeling was that of fear because Sophie always wondered when it would be her turn to be chosen to die.

During puberty, Sophie developed an addiction to pain and would harm herself by pulling out her nails or cutting the soles of her feet so that she had to walk around on bleeding feet. As she grew older, she reflected on her condition and realized that she had no self-love, only pain. So barren was her emotional landscape, that she resorted to drastic measures to feel anything, and the easiest route was to cause herself pain.

The Chateau Des Armois is a castle located in the Ardennes Forest in the southeast of Belgium. The Mothers of Darkness, as it became known, is shrouded in mystery and until the last two decades, has remained largely secret to the general public. Its location was even hidden on satellite imagery. The English title came from researchers who posited that high level Illuminati witches and Satanic priestesses would be trained at the castle using MK Ultra techniques. Candidates —which included daughters and granddaughters — would be subjected to unimaginable abuse as children. Repeated trauma is a primary causal factor for dissociative identity disorder, which makes it easier to program the children.

Chateau Des Armois, or sometimes known as Castle of Kings, is owned by Alice Solvay whose uncle was Ernest Solvay, founder of the Belgian multinational chemical and pharmaceutical company. They invented Prozac and drinkable fluoride. There are numerous online reports and Youtube videos in circulation which allege that the Mothers of Darkness castle was used as a central European location for Satanists, Illuminati, and their invited guests. Within the stone walls, guests would participate in pedophilic evenings, child sacrifice, and initiation ceremonies. On the gated grounds of the estate, hunting parties would assemble, but not to hunt for deer or boar or fox, but children. Adults, and often children themselves, would hunt down and kill other children for sport, in a grotesquely similar fashion to the movie *Hunger Games*.

You might be surprised that organizations as fraternal as the secret societies would have a women's auxiliary such as the Mothers of Darkness witches, but let me remind you that women participated in these dark and debaucherous practices just as much as the men did. The twin snakes of the caduceus symbol represent binaries, male and female, wrapped around a wand. This symbology is found on the stomach of the Baphomet statue at the Satanic temple in Detroit and many other illustrations. It represents magic, spiritual enlightenment, wisdom, immortality, and healing. When a man and woman combine to perform sexual magic for the purposes of creating a child, it is god-like and blessed. When the same forces combine sexual magic to desecrate and destroy a child, then it is of the opposite polarity, and a complete inversion of natural and cosmic law.

There is a fine line between legend and fact surrounding Chateau Des Armois. The BBC and National Geographic have allegedly been denied access, so there remains a sense of secrecy which fuels deeper speculation. Privately funded researchers have attempted to film and investigate the location, but have been turned away by security patrols, rolls of barbed wire, electric fences, and trip wires. All that seems somewhat excessive to maintain a level of privacy. Youtube content and conspiracy theories aside, the most well-known research into this castle was conducted after witnesses from the Dutroux case specifically named the site. The book *Les X-Dossiers* by Anne-Mie Bulte, Douglas Coninck, Marie-Jeanne Van Heeswyck, cite several witnesses who have confirmed allegations of what took place there and the various notables who attended. In the first pages of the book, there is a list of accused persons from the Dutroux case, the Maud Sarr and Les Ballets Roses. The list is replete with politicians, police, doctors, and royalty.

Astute researchers linked comments made by US President H.W Bush when he referred to *1000 points of light* in several speeches. There is a room within the castle where evil rituals were performed under the glass domed ceiling where 1000 points of light shine down to the floor beneath. It's alleged that President H.W Bush took his two daughters there to be initiated into evil.

In isolation, these connections may seem tenuous, and the stories magnified, but when they are corroborated by survivors of Satanic ritual abuse networks, and the professionals like Carine who fight in the trenches of that war, then we have enough congruency to start drawing firm conclusions. Sophie has spoken to survivors from the castle and to the local Belgian special forces police unit to confirm their statements. Research into the castle began in earnest in the early 1990's and thirty years later there is little talk of it. Some have speculated that there is a lot of DNA evidence within the walls of European castles which is slowly being burned off, and that due to the huge volume of publicity that Chateaux Des Armois received, the organization has relocated its operations to more secluded sites.

You may think that I've passed you a bottle of blood spiked Kool Aid, but I assure you that the people who were interviewed for this chapter are real. Their stories are real. Aside from the single name I've falsified to protect Sophie, you are welcome to research all of them yourself. But what is the point of all this? I know you detect the presence of a menacing darkness in this world, and you see its blood-soaked fingerprints in the crime scenes of every evil deed. We know evil men by the fruits of their deeds. You see absolute abuse of power and a decay in cosmic natural law. Inversions permeate our lives and the media we consume so freely and easily at our fingertips is delivered by artificial intelligences whose customized algorithms, predictability indexes and IQs are orders of magnitude higher than ours. Absent morality, the animal instincts of men can act freely, and with each negative choice we slip deeper into the abyss. Do you feel society slipping? Are there any taboos remaining beyond the rebadging of a pedophile to a minor attracted person?

The disturbing revelation of swallowing this red pill, is that the devil didn't do it, man did. Nothing can happen in this material world, without the agency of man, and the exercising of his free will. Unchecked, man has a rapacious gluttony and unquenchable thirst for power and wealth and control. The governments, organizations and secret societies that form around these codes of conduct are growing. Men and women seal their memberships in these organizations by the very acts of sacrifice and perversion which entangle them. There is a free choice for the individual to seek power, healing, regeneration, or money. Once you are in, it is nearly impossible to escape.

The battlegrounds between good and evil are within the confines of humans. Carl Jung was right, every one of us has a shadow self which requires integration. This does not mean you have carte blanche to go and do whatever you want, but it is important that you understand and are aware of that darker shadow aspect within yourself, and that you are morally forearmed before a tantalizing transaction is offered to you. Before you judge consider this: If the devil sat beside you as he did with Christ in the desert, and offered you that which you most desired, could you resist? If ultimate power and darkness was your friend, and you needed a problem solved, could you resist? As Carine says, *there are so many people asleep at the wheel, and their minds are in a state of delusion and desperation*. They're lulled by mass media and the antianxiety and antidepressant medication they consume. Spiritual warfare is a war of inches. It's a game to capture your soul. The more you choose the darker option and give in to immoral temptation, the darker you become until you have completely lost your soul and you've become like one of the monsters standing in the circle around the altar. You may not be committing these explicit acts yourself, but your inaction in the face of evil might as well be conspiracy. Now that you know these things, you cannot be apathetic towards it. Inaction is bystander behavior.

Chapter 8

Blood

It's really quite impossible to understand what's going on in the world if you don't understand blood. It's a bloody mess, what with the nonsense in the witchcraft and the Satanism, but I'll bet nobody has ever taken the time to explain it all to you. Worry not, now is your time.

Blood is a powerful cohesive between this world and the next, or, more specifically, the physical and the astral. It might seem like an odd place to begin a narrative on blood, but the most direct relationship we get between blood and the negative principality is from Goethe in his classic two-part poem, Faust. In the epic narrative, Dr Faust enters into a contract with an entity by the name of *Mephistopheles*, an agent of the devil or the devil himself depending on interpretation. We get the following exchange.

Mephistopheles

> Why launch into oratory too?
> Hot-tempered: you exaggerate as well.
> Any bit of paper's just as good.
> And you can sign it with a drop of blood.

Faust

If it will satisfy you, and it should,
Then let's complete the farce in full.

Mephistopheles

Blood is a quite special fluid.

If you're part of the Western world and its cultural and religious traditions, you might have noticed the role that blood plays. The central sacrament of the Catholic mass is the consumption of the body and blood. This, of course, refers to the body and blood of Jesus Christ. Having been born to a Catholic family, I could never quite understand this ritual. It was explained to me numerous times by priests, my parents, my grandmothers, and even a bishop once, but I still couldn't understand it. I mean, come on, some guy's blood is going to save me from damnation? The words didn't escape me. I've always been proficient with English, just the concept, the transcendent concept, plus, of course, the obvious question, what does some Jew in Roman occupied Jerusalem have to do with me, a Canadian of Scottish ethnicity, a tribe who themselves battled the Romans and were declared uncivilized as memorialized on Hadrian's Wall. We were a lot like the Jews, and Hadrian's Wall was built around the same time the Second Temple of Solomon was destroyed. Adding curiosity is the fact that both Hadrian's Wall and the Wailing Wall, or Western Wall of the Second Temple, which the Romans left standing, are both UNESCO Heritage Sites. Even more curious, I live in and wrote this book from a UNESCO Heritage Site, the Talamanca Mountains, where I live in Costa Rica, next to a Cabecare native reserve. If you study your life closely enough you will see your past lives, and you will see all the karmic connections in your life. You don't have to go into a hypnotic trance, or spend money on some flake claiming to be an akashic record reader. It's all right in front of you. You just haven't developed the ability to see it.

The Jews were more advanced than us. The weather in the Middle-East and the access to all kinds of rich cultures like Egypt, Babylon, and Phoenicia gave them a rich library of cultural information, including some pretty dark stuff on blood. Jerusalem was an early instance of multiculturalism, like my birth country of Canada and the city of Toronto where I spent most of my adult life. It has more languages spoken than any other city in the world. Rome was also multicultural. The Jews had their own language, culture, and religion, and so did the Scots. We spoke Gaelic and our religion was Druidism, a highly advanced system of prayer, ritual, invocation, and self-development. Rome was the Amazon of its day, and Scotland and Israel were family owned businesses trying to get by. You see what I mean about things never really changing, how the past is the present, and you just need eyes to see it? Druids performed human sacrifices, usually criminals, and they adjudicated all disputes. Their training was quite intense, sometimes twenty years, and they were alleged to possess transcendent powers. Some take them back to the Tuatha Dé Danann, the Celtic gods associated with Ireland. Myth has them coming in on a mist. The truth is the mist was an effect created by the portal they came through. Many of the myths of the past will be metaphysically explained when the pall of malignant monotheism leaves the human race, and it doesn't have much longer. Portals are explained in *Stardust Ranch: The Incredible True Story*. All these things were understood and preserved, even in the near past, until the twentieth century and the devil's plan.

I always felt alien to the Catholic Church and its doctrine. I just couldn't understand the concept behind the Eucharist. How could the consumption *in effigy* of a dead spiritual figure be seen as anything other than the vile practice I have always seen it as? But it gets worse. Blood is really central to the whole Abrahamic story. It goes right back to the beginning. No judgment on my part, as I come from a line that burned people alive in a straw man, as depicted in the film, *The Wicker Man*, and I highly recommend the original 1973 British version with Edward Woodward, not the insufferable American remake with Nicolas Cage. The Catholic Church stole the Jewish culture, grafted themselves onto it, and brought everyone under their mind control empire, the empire that could operate largely without shields and swords. Romans loved cultural appropriation. Julius Ceasar was enthralled with the Druids, grabbed himself a couple priests in battle and brought them to Rome, but the Jews got royally fucked in the siege of Jerusalem, and, as far as I can tell, it was just their geographic position that made them vulnerable and desirable. Scotland and Ireland were at the other end of the European land mass, and the terrain of the Highlands made them like the Taliban of their day, unbeatable when they fought as guerilla units, the Picts charging out of the mist naked and painted. Imagine that.

Before the *blood of Christ* there was just blood.

Genesis 4:3-24

> Cain brought to the LORD an offering of the fruit of the ground
> Abel also brought of the firstborn of his flock and of their fat portions
> And the LORD had regard for Abel and his offering, but for Cain and his offering he had no regard

Now, if you're so inclined, and you dig deeper into the theological interpretation of this passage, some will say that Abel's offering was one in which he *gave up* more. I suppose you could make the case that by market prices the fatty parts of freshly slaughtered animals would be more valuable than fruit — the vegan crowd has certainly ridiculously elevated the price of avocado — but the problem comes into play when you look at the larger context of spirituality as a planetary phenomenon. Most spiritual paths advocate vegetarianism. Some of the more austere advocate pure veganism, and they suggest that even small portions of animal products in the body will dilute the contemplative experience for deep meditators. Certainly, the commandment not to kill is everywhere in religion. The Hindus have made a sacred animal out of the cow because of the non meat food it provides in the form of dairy products. The Buddha recommends that initiates do not eat meat that was slaughtered *specifically* for them, but, because the path depends upon the life of a mendicant, if in the course of begging a mendicant monk is offered meat he or she should eat it. However, if you're preparing your own diet as an ordained Buddhist monk, and buying all your groceries or growing and preparing all your own food, then no meat is preferred. This is what's so strange about the book of Genesis in the Bible. Right from the get-go we're introduced to a god that likes things killed for it, and, more specifically, blood.

So what's up with blood? To understand blood you have to delve into the texts of the secret societies in the Western tradition. It's important to understand that when you look at the available texts for the masses in the religion of Abraham and his descendants, the principal documents are the worker class theology. The management class theology is in the secret societies. The mother of all secret societies and secret teachings is the Kabbalah, although it was originally reserved just for Jews. However, it did manage to creep out into gentile culture once Protestantism was formed. It went by the name Freemasonry. I wrote about this in *The Light of Darkness: A Warrior's Tale for our Time*.

The Kabbalah found expression in most of the European secret societies that were oppositional to the Vatican and were, prior to the advancement of the enlightenment and the Protestant Reformation, quite illegal, and illegal under Vatican rule meant the most demonically imagined tortures or slow and painful death, and let me take moment to say here that the most heinous religious expression I know of is my birth religion of Catholicism. It brings us right back to the blood, too, doesn't it? The blood of Christ cleanses sins. Christ opened the world of Jewish blood sacrifice to everyone. The Jews hate this, and justifiably so. It usurped their authority over a cannon of religious literature which had been meticulously maintained by the rabbis for centuries, and it has to be noted that Jewish culture maintained a high degree of literacy at a time when most of the world was illiterate. Jews are far from perfect, and they may well be responsible for introducing the blood rituals and sex rituals which dominate the world Carine Hustebaut introduced us to in this book, but make no mistake about it, the greater enemy of man was and always has been the Vatican. I am baptized and confirmed in this faith, confirmed by no less than Archbishop Plourd in Ottawa in 1978, but I was thinking outside of it by the time I was seventeen. Catholicism smelled rotten to me right from the beginning. I don't know why some people can think outside of their birth culture. Most people fit into it like water into a cup. If the culture says strap a bomb on and blow yourself up in a shopping mall screaming

Allahhu Akbar then you do it, no questions asked. Somehow I knew culture was a scam. Sure, aspects of it can be true, but the larger concept of culture was a scam.

Blood is the *river of life* in the esoteric sense. It connects two worlds, the world of elementary spirit, or the astral plane, and the physical world. Blood can very much be compared in its utility and function in the body to chlorophyll and the role it plays in the plant kingdom. Curiously, it has been suggested in the exopolitics community that chlorophyll plays a role in the functioning of the bodies of the small gray aliens which infected and invaded Stardust Ranch. This was the general conclusion of Doctor Levengood when he studied the tissue samples from the gray alien John Edmonds sent him. He said the biological sample showed more in common with plants than mammals, despite the tissue coming from a bipedal hominid, a small gray alien. Even more curious, Edmonds told me that he could draw the grays out by smearing menstrual blood in the house or garage, and that they would almost inadvertently show up in short time. I didn't put this in the book. It was one of the many things I learned from John.

Another constituent of blood is what becomes and produces the hormone secretions of glands. This comes to play a large role in the Adrenochrome market.

> Adrenochrome is a chemical compound produced by the oxidation of adrenaline (epinephrine). It was the subject of limited research from the 1950s through to the 1970s as a potential cause of schizophrenia. While it has no current medical application, the related derivative compound, carbazochrome, is a hemostatic medication.

Adrenochrome is the urban myth that won't stay down in the

conspiracy world. It's been around for a while, much longer than most people realize. It first publicly appears in *Fear and Loathing in Las Vegas*, the seminal work of Gonzo journalism that established Hunter S Thompson as a cultural force to be reckoned with in the post hippie world of America.

> "Take a hit out of that little brown bottle in my shaving kit."
>
> "What is it?"
>
> "Adrenochrome," he said. "You won't need much. Just a little tiny taste."
>
> I got the bottle and dipped the head of a paper match into it.
>
> "That's about right," he said. "That stuff makes pure mescaline seem like ginger beer. You'll go completely crazy if you take too much."
>
> I licked the end of the match. "Where'd you get this?" I asked. "You can't buy it."
>
> "Never mind," he said. "It's absolutely pure."
>
> I shook my head sadly. "Jesus! What kind of monster client have you picked up this time? There's only one source for this stuff . . ."
>
> He nodded.
>
> "The adrenaline glands from a living human body," I said. "It's no good if you get it out of a corpse."
>
> "I know," he replied. "But the guy didn't have any cash. He's one of these Satanism freaks. He offered me human blood—said it would make me higher than I'd ever been in my life," he laughed. "I thought he was kidding, so I told him I'd just as soon have an ounce or so

> of pure adrenochrome—or maybe just a fresh adrenalin gland to chew on."

Adrenochrome is alleged by many whistle blowers to be the drug of choice for the ritual set, and some suggest it's where a lot of the missing children are going, tortured and terrified to produce the best adrenal secretion in the blood. It sounds like the stuff of a terrible horror movie yet to be made, but it's all too real, kept out of the public consciousness by a society too frightened to speak about it, except in the darkest corners of the Internet. But, hands down, the greatest utility for blood is magic. It is one of the currencies of magic, like money, gold, or silver in the world. This topic was addressed in *The Light of Darkness: A Warriors Tale for our Time*. In that book I examined the religion of Palo Mayombe, which my co-author, Robert Wiegand, initiated into. It's in a class of religious traditions alongside Santeria and Voodoo. The religion originated in the Congo and focuses on the spirits of the dead. Blood is a central offering in the religion. The priests, known as Tatas, sacrifice blood on their altars, which are usually set off in a separate room, like a work shed or cabin, or a special part of the house. Sometimes the Tata will share his body with the spirits, and drink alcohol and smoke cigars, so that the deceased spirits can enjoy the libations as well. It's not quite channeling and not quite possession, but, rather, a controlled occupation, and, when the Tata is occupied, as the spirit is enjoying the body, the Tata can experience the spirit world, see things at different points of time and space, what magicians sometimes call remote viewing. The blood offerings usually focus on chickens or goats or small mammals.

The metaphysical is a form of physics, the perfect blend of art and science among the best practitioners, but, thanks to the twentieth century, the collapse of the spiritual imagination, and the corralling of human consciousness into black box rationality, people who talk about these things seem irrational, deranged, and quite possibly schizophrenic, so not many people talk about them, at least not in public. Of course the Masons, Rosicrucians, Martinists, Gnostics, Vedic practitioners of the left and right hand paths, Jesuits, and Kabbalists all know exactly what I'm talking about, so long as they didn't quit before getting a few degrees or sufficient sadhana.

And now it's time to deal with the elephant in the room, the Jews, their religion, traditions, and the special place that blood has in the root of the Abrahamic system. As already stated in this book, most of what we're told is Jewish, is not. It's a sad fact of the human race that most people can't tell you what happened right in front of them. Ask any detective who interviews people for witness testimony. Human perception is extremely fragile and unreliable. Map that out over decades and centuries and millennia and the probability that you're getting things right is almost non-existent. We know that the Jews sacrificed animals. The question then is, can sin be atoned for with the sacrifice of animals? What is sin? It's a transgression against god, or against spiritual law. This begs the question, what is spiritual law? It depends who is answering the question. The Jews are the legal department of the religious set. No religion in the world has codified more than the Jews. This penchant for law influenced the Western world quite a bit, especially after the enlightenment. Most of the economic law we have has been greatly influenced by Jews. The first major central bank was The Bank of England. It was set up by Jews. Both money and blood are currencies. Money buys things in this world. Blood buys things in the astral world. The simplest way to explain all of this is economy.

Imagine you have a dog. You live on a farm. When you go to sleep at night the dog is your protection. It will bark if anything comes near the farm house. It will attack anything it feels might threaten the humans who tend to it. And what does tending the dog look like? It's feeding the dog. You take care of the dog and the dog takes care of you. It's no different with blood offerings. The only question is what is consuming the blood? Any number of things is the simple and direct answer. The Chinese have the concept of hungry ghosts. It's not just a concept, they actually exist. There are many forms of hell on the other side. One of these hells is a realm close to this one in which all the needs of the body persist, needs like hunger, thirst, desire for alcohol, tobacco, and other things, even sex. The kind of spirit that exists in this state is a hungry ghost. The state is a karmic punishment. It can go on for quite some time. There are forms of magic which can feed these ghosts, some white magic, performed out of compassion by benevolent and enlightened beings, usually monks or some other class of deep spiritual practitioner, and some black magic, performed to compel and control the hungry ghosts, usually by Satanists or some other nefarious group with knowledge of the dimensions.

The state a person occupies in the afterlife is dependant on the energy they cultivated in this life. If a person spends their whole life intoxicated and they die suddenly, they can find themselves in this hungry ghost state. The word hungry denotes the continued craving for things of the body. There are loads of these entities in bars. The alcoholics are easy access for them, and they can share the consciousness of the drunkard and enjoy the alcohol. This isn't possession. It's more like cohabitation. If this situation persists for an extended period, the openings in the aura caused by alcohol intoxication may potentially become lasting or permanent, and then the person may very well become possessed, but that's such a difficult word because it always conjures the demonic legions due to religious misunderstanding. The truth is most possessions which imbalance a person are dead human beings, not demons.

There are many multidimensional economies. Blood is perhaps the most diabolical. The energy in blood is a food on the lower astral, a drug, a whiskey, or any other such analogy as the cultural association might affix, so long as you get the point. Blood gets attention on the other side. Getting the attention of entities on the other side is one dimension of the black magician's task, the next task is communicating your will to them.

Let's circle back to the tribe, the Jews. Are these ancient blood practices part of any economy we could associate with god? Absolutely not. We've come too far as a human culture, shared too much through the decades and hours of work translating sacred texts. There is no misunderstanding in the universal world of consciousness. No god in existence craves blood or compels adherents to spill blood, unless you consider what the Aztecs were worshiping to be god. These blood entities have been flirting with human beings for quite some time. Stories abound in the occult. But one thing is certain, they are not god, not the primal cause, the one true and loving creator of all the realities seen and unseen. The principal characteristic of god is love, unconditional love. This is what we get from the Buddhists, though they give no form to a god, rather a field of energy and state of realization that is permanent and compassionate. It is more or less the same in Hinduism, though they have many gods who act as intermediaries to the amorphous divine. Islam has ritual holidays in which an animal is sacrificed to feed the poor, but the idea of blood for atonement does not exist.

The Jews, however, have always had a very special, and, quite frankly, magical and occult relationship with blood, and the dark inner circle of the Jews, the Satanic Zionists, want to not only bring back the Third Temple of Solomon but all of the blood offerings to their god, which, according to them wants blood, and wants no other religions to exist in the world. This day of reckoning with the formidable Jews, the darkest of black magicians on the planet, is at hand and will almost certainly be seen in this living generation.

There is little to no doubt in my mind that it is these Jews who introduced the Satanic rituals Carine Hustebaut came to understand in her journey down the child sacrifice and ritual abuse rabbit hole. It's a horrible journey she has made, and one I made while writing *The Light of Darkness* with Robert Wiegand. It amazes me that people can still doubt this reality, or its genesis in the Jewish community, but, due to the unfortunate fate of European Jews in the Second World War, any mention of the Jews and their bloody relationship with the demonic realm is immediately relegated to anti-Semitism. Forget that the larger holocaust was the Germans ritually sacrificed to the sum of eight million, rounded up into concentration camps, raped, tortured and starved. If you don't know about that you might want to ask yourself why. The simple answer is the victor writes the history, and the official narrative is that the Nazis lost the war, but, as we look at all the oddities noted in the *1947* chapter of this book, even that is debatable. It seems, horrible as it sounds, that the Nazis and Zionists are one entity, and, in the early part of the twenty-first century, working together for the depopulation of the planet. It's important to note, once again, that all the evidence suggests that the Jews are not the Zionists and the Germans are not the Nazis. I think both groups have morphed into a transhuman perversion, and, most certainly, the authors of the end times we seem to be living through which masquerade as prophecy. It's not a prophecy. It's a plan.

The blood, of course, goes back to The Temple of Solomon. It's a question of debate whether King Solomon actually existed as a historical figure, and whether the first temple actually existed, but the lore is a fascinating insight into the time and into the secret societies which revere Solomon, the great builder. If we want to make an extraterrestrial connection, the magic and blood letting in the temple is reptilian. It's interesting to note that Jewish activist groups managed to get David Icke, the British writer and modern exponent of the reptilian presence on the planet, labeled as an anti-Semite. Equally curious is the official world's response to the reptilian theory. They think it's batshit nuts. But is it? All major Eastern religions reference the naga, who were — yeah, you guessed it — shape shifting reptilian humanoids. Even Buddha described them extensively in his sutras, exactly and quite literally as David Icke described them.

The Temple of Solomon is a feeding center. There is no atonement for sin in these barbaric rituals. They are feeding and directing very dark entities. And what do these entities do? They affect the physical plane. Think of any ghost story you know about, one in which one or a small group of dead people haunt and torment a region for ages. What do you get? You get inexplicable physical phenomenon, things moving, levitating, doors opening and closing, bad dreams, negative emotions, perhaps even suicidal feelings. Amp that up several orders of magnitude and you are beginning to understand The Temple of Solomon magic. It's not meant to help humanity or provide a legitimate space for worship among true celebrants of god, no, not at all, more like a throne for a negative principality of immense power. This is what the Christian Zionists don't understand. They can't see the scope of it, the supernatural nature of multigenerational planning. They just can't see it. They are unwittingly bringing in this darkness because they have been led to believe it will herald the return of Christ, the most hated Jewish apostate in the Talmud, a soul stewing in boiling feces for all eternity according to the rabbis. The hatred is the mark of their perversion. These racist Jews, these chosen people of god, cannot abide their not ruling the world with the rest of us as their slaves. It's pure evil. It's the same evil that stains the stones of the Mother of Darkness castle in Belgium, the same evil that has been creeping through Europe since Martin Luther, the Presbyterians, and the Anglican Church, all Jewish religions despite paying lip service to Christ.

How could this evil have festered and grown for three and a half centuries you might ask? How could we have not seen it when it now seems so manifest and obvious? A horrible and demonic figure like Sabbatai Levi gets named the messiah in 1666, a group of Amsterdam Jews wins the charter for The Bank of England, Freemasonry suddenly starts to proliferate in England and Scotland at the same time, and secret societies springing off the Kabbalah emerge all through Europe, and nobody can put the pieces together? It's preposterous. The bravest voice I've seen in this arena is, in fact, a Jew, who, by the way, the cult has no problem killing, despite the facade of unity among the Jews. Any Torah Jew who was brave enough to tell the truth would disappear, perhaps along with his family. It's not Jewish. It's not the religion of Abraham. It's demonic, blood lusting, black magic Satanism, the ultimate apostate to Abraham's love of the creator, and the triumph of the forces of darkness that Abraham stood against, so let's stop the pretense that this is Jewish. Zionism is demonic, as was Nazism. Let's get our history right. Let's get our theology right. Let's get our truth right.

Perhaps the most damning testament of the connection between blood offerings and black magic and the Jewish Community comes from a Sephardic Jew by the name of Dr Ariel Toaff, a professor of Medieval and Renaissance History at Bar-Ilan University in Israel, whose work has focused on Jews and their history in Italy. It's very rare that a Jew speaks against the Jews. Whatever conscience they have concerning the fate of the *goyim* is not shared with the goyim. In 2007 he published a book called *Blood Passover: The Jews of Europe and Ritual Murder*. It was very promptly banned by no other than the Anti-Defamation League (ADL). The author is a professor in Israel and the son of the head rabbi in Rome.

It should be noted that the professor seems to be directing most of his assertions at a subset of Jews, who, despite being numerically superior in the twenty-first century, do not represent the totality of Judaica, and here I'm referring to the Ashkenazi Jews. They are the dominant force in Israel now. Their history is connected to Ukraine and Germany, and they are the creators of the Yiddish language. They do not represent the totality of the Jewish population worldwide.

The professor speaks multiple languages, including Italian and German, the two languages necessary to survey the records of one of the most infamous blood libel cases in European history, the case of one little Simon of Trent. Like so many other cases alleged by countries that hosted diaspora Jews, it has been labeled anti-Semitism by the Jewish establishment and the various bodies of Jewish defense which populate Western countries, but it's the professor's assertion that it actually happened, and he goes to painstaking lengths to make his case. It would be very difficult for any reasonable person to read the evidence and not conclude that Ashkenazi Jews ritually murdered this little boy, though the usual figures and bodies have emerged to rebuke the work. The Jews have a special label for these kinds of people, *self-hating Jews*.

Perhaps it could be said that much of the suspicion of Jews is in fact anti-Semitism. I have already confessed my loathing of my birth religion, Catholicism, and so I, like professor Toaff, have committed the sin of turning on my tribe, but not really. I side with the Jews here. The church is Rome, and Rome the theological empire is every bit as chauvinistic and bullying as Rome the sword and shield empire. They are the elitists of the elitists, psychopathic in their lust for power and aggrandizement in the eyes of their fellow Europeans, and, quite frankly, despicable in their utility of Yeshua of Nazareth as their claim to authority. Rome is not my tribe. The Celts are my tribe, the Tuatha De Danann my original gods, in the Hindu sense, meaning the multidimensional star travelers who seeded me here as a soul experience, and make no mistake about it, Shiva and his *blue gods* were just that, star beings.

The truth is, as I see it now, both the Sanhedrin and the Vatican are despicable in their pursuit of the control of humanity, either by force, theology, abusive usury, or black magic. They are the same. Both are the enemies of mankind, as are the bearded fanatics in Mecca who believe Muhammed and his caliphate should rule the world. How did we get this stupid? It's hard to know. To say we got this stupid is to suggest we once knew better, and there doesn't seem to be a whole lot of evidence for that.

Getting back to blood in the concrete, devoid of speculation, its purpose and power, let me now explain the meaning of sacrifice in the Jewish religion. It took place in the temple. It was conducted by a high priest. The inner chamber of the temple was reserved for the high priest. He had to be absolutely pure, though, I must confess, I don't know what pure means by Jewish definition, nor do I really care, save to understand it's nothing which I would call pure.

An important distinction is required here. Like all things, Judaica has changed and evolved over the years. Many Jews alive today in the diaspora, living lives of observance within Reform Judaism or other forms of liberalized Judaism, find the blood work as antiquated and repugnant as non-Jews, and, atop this mild distinction in Judaica, there is also the great line — Satanism and Judaism. It cannot be argued that a portion of the Jewish community has degenerated into outright Satanism, demonic communion, vile blood ritual, human torture, and ritual murder, but it's not just them anymore. Many non-Jews have found their way into this Satanic religion by blackmail, gradual alignment with it through graduation into the higher degrees of Kabbalah inspired secret societies like Freemasonry, Rosicrucianism, Martinism, and others, not to mention the spread of various forms of pagan witchcraft which survived independent of Jewish apostasy but which have certainly benefited, risen with the tide of black magic which seems to be omnipresent now, but the root of it, and the master practitioners are the Jews. If you doubt what I am telling you, ask a black magician. They'll tell you.

These rituals we see in places of power, all over the world, including Washington, not just the Europe to which Carine introduced us, the human trafficking, the child trafficking, it's all part of a larger system within our systems. It's not the totality of anything. Illuminated Torah Jews exist, illuminated by god. There are judges and police and bankers at the top levels who stand outside these blasphemies against the creator, but they watch helplessly as the system to which they swore allegiance is more and more corrupted with the passing decades. It only takes a very small fraction of these Satanists to corrupt a larger population. The darker the individual practitioner the more complete the infection of the system with which they interact, usually at a management level.

Now let's start putting some things together. The extraterrestrial phenomenon is directly linked to Israel and Jewish black magic. The rituals open portals. There are many things out there, many, many things. The gods of our religions are almost always beings from other races and dimensions. Shiva is a blue Sirian from the Sirius star system. The prophets are part Pleidian and part Anunnaki, the people of Nibiru. Most of our teachings originate from beyond this planet.

There is a strong correlation between the Jews, The Temple of Solomon, and the UFO movement. As noted in the *1947* chapter, both Israel and Roswell happen in 1947. The official formation of Israel is 1948, but the bloody work to get it secured by the European Jews dropped off by the British Navy after World War II is 1947, then curiously, during the Yom Kippur War of 1973 we get the year of the UFO. The spike in UFO activity in 1973 is enormous. And it's not just Israel. This has to do with the temple. Remember, the Temple of Solomon was built by demons, which, in the analogy given already in this book, meet the definition of extraterrestrial. They love word games, these negative practitioners. You see, there really is a god, and it must be respected. It can best be described as the life field, or the field within which life can happen, on all planes and dimensions. There are rules. Because good people have been swayed by humanism and forgotten the truth of god and gods, we have allowed this magical nonsense and demonology or negative extraterrestrial crap to get out of hand, after all, how do you convince people something is going on if the context for understanding it, religion and spirituality, has been decimated? You're a laughing stock. People who understand by personal experience what I have written about in this trilogy — *Stardust Ranch: The Incredible True Story, The Light of Darkness: A Warrior's Tale for our Time*, and this final tome — can't thank me enough. Those who don't understand think I need to be medicated and institutionalized, but it doesn't matter. My family and neighbors in my small Spanish pueblo in the Talamanca Mountains know nothing about the books — save my wife because the paranormal phenomenon that attends the writing of these books is phenomenal — nor do I even try to explain, so my life is peaceful and relaxed.

Magic and orbs and portals and apparitions have always gone together, and, while true extraterrestrials do exist, as in humanoids from other planets and star systems, the vast majority of what we are talking about today is related to magic, and it is intentional. Most of that magic is coming from the dark Jewish world, and much of it is to serve as a distraction so people do not make the connection between the blood thirsty Temple of Solomon and UFOs. The abductions are a part of it as well. There's a book that explains a lot about the utility of magic, the appearance of orbs and paranormal phenomenon, and the migration of the Jewish diaspora in Europe. The Israel project and the Third Temple have been in play for centuries now. That book is *The Gods of Eden* by William Bramley. I also feel the need to say some things that were not in *Stardust Ranch: The Incredible True Story*. John Edmonds and I became good friends, and we spoke all the time. He was one of the most fascinating people you could pass three hours with. John was born into this ruling cabal that owns the Western world. He was a first generation super soldier. If you don't know anything about the super soldier program, it was an ancillary program to MK Ultra and the various mind control programs that proliferated after the Second World War. There's a war going they have not told us, the general public about, probably for fear it would send us into a panic. The war is happening outside the frequencies of our reality, and by frequencies I mean the light and sound spectrum visible within our senses, but that's just the beginning. Life and experience go on way beyond these limited human faculties. This is a big part of the UFO world, the abductions, and so much of what is just beyond our grasp. We've been trying to grab onto this for some time now, and it's like trying to grab steam with your hand, but it's all coming into focus now, thanks to the Satanic push for the Third Temple of Solomon.

John told me a lot of things about the gray aliens he experienced at the ranch, and, though he never admitted it to me, I think he was assigned to Stardust Ranch, as a kind of steward, a protector of the human race. What was going on at that ranch, and still is as far as I know, is diabolical. It was a smuggling route for extraterrestrials. What do they smuggle you might ask? Us. We are the prize, our genetics, our DNA, and our blood. DNA has a role in spirituality we haven't quite understood yet, at least not at the level of public discourse. It's a bridge between the main levels of unfoldment, the chemical and manifest world — the sulfur, mercury, and salt of the alchemists and yogis — and the higher parts of us, which are purely spiritual, refining into higher and higher frequencies of sound and light, which is the true voice of god, until we go beyond even the sound and light and go to a place that has no sound but is not silent and has no light but is not dark, and it starts with incarnation and DNA.

John is known as the *alien killer*. People laughed at me when I wrote the book — some people — but those in the know quietly cheered. He explained everything to me. He tried all kinds of ways to kill them. It wasn't until the samurai sword came into his possession that he figured it out. You have to decapitate the motherfuckers. And so he did. But how do you sneak up on something that can phase out of this reality, literally disappear, and do it with limbs chopped off, fuelled by a chlorophyll blood system like a living plant, darting between the third and fourth dimensions like a gopher coming out of and going into a tunnel system? Well, like every hunter, you have to know how to bait your prey, bring it in to your tree stand, where you're waiting with your rifle, your crossbow, or, in this case, your samurai sword. So how did he bait them? He smeared human menstrual blood on fabrics, like the seat of a motorcycle in the garage, then waited. Are you starting to understand what I'm trying to tell you?

Chapter 9

The Event Horizon

The things that I say in this book are shocking — I know that — especially if you're coming in cold, and by *cold* I mean none of the threads I have pulled on were known to you prior to encountering them in this book. Part of me wants to apologize, to say sorry for making you aware of these things, but, to be honest, fuck you for being asleep at the spiritual wheel of your life. We're in this together as a society, and if your low consciousness, your lack of awareness can be used to create a more Satanic and Draconian society because you're too stupid, too lazy, or too distracted by your own self-interest and pleasures to give a fuck, then you're a big part of the problem.

If absolutely none of the things described in this book were known to you, then the fault lies with you. It means that your inner being is so diminished that you've forgotten how to feel correctly. I'm not *trying* to make you feel bad, but you should feel bad. That *bad feeling* is evidence that you exist as a spiritual being, but that's the triumph of the twentieth century, is it not? That's why the opening chapter of this middle part of the book is called *Our Last Free Breath*. You see, all of this has been done intentionally. This is an incredibly difficult thing for people to comprehend in a secular age because our definition of evil rarely goes beyond the avarice and malice of a single human being in a single human life. Through our now secular philosophy and humanism we can easily understand the corrupt nature of Mao or Stalin or several other minor and major despots who have populated recent history. Human beings are corruptible. Power is the ultimate intoxicant. This is the theology of humanism, and we all understand it and we all speak about it. How could any group of people maintain such discipline over centuries and generations? If you really have to ask that question after reading the book thus far then there's not much I can do to help you. What do you think the trauma-based conditioning is about? What do you think inter-generational Satanism is about? What do you think the child murdering is about? What do you think the sex rituals are about? Are you really going to pretend these things aren't going on? Is it still easier for you to believe that I'm crazy? Or are you finally ready to accept the predicament that we are in as a human race? It is the eleventh hour, and people have no idea of the danger all about us. How does that happen? It's inbred into us as biological beings. It has taken tremendous effort to program us this way, and it's all been done in such a way that we didn't even know it was being done.

You may say to yourself how could such a widespread conspiracy exist without you having heard of it? The answer is simple. The conspiracy is an operative system. The vast majority of participants in the conspiracy are unconscious. This is why the spiritual consciousness had to be collapsed. The plan would only work with unconscious people, and that unconsciousness was created with us en masse the same way it is accomplished on an individual, mind control through trauma. Would you believe me if I told you that many of the serial killers let loose upon American society were trained and deployed by America's own intelligence agencies? This is the widespread understanding of Charles Manson, thanks to numerous podcasters who have done hundreds if not thousands of hours of research, and, of course, the spellbinding *Chaos: Charles Manson, the CIA, and the Secret History of the Sixties*, by Tom O'Neill, a Vanity Fair freelancer who spent two decades on the book. The work is supported by writers like Dave McGowan in *Weird Scenes Inside the Canyon: Laurel Canyon, Covert Ops & the Dark Heart of the Hippie Dream* which chronicles the relationship between military intelligence, the CIA, and the music scene in Laurel Canyon, but not even O'Neill or McGowan go into the Satanic underbelly. That's where it all comes together. None of it really makes sense until the rituals are understood.

Satanism is why we had to go to rational humanism and shut down the awakened imagination of the divine self and the awakened human. This is why the spiritual state of the West is so dilapidated, and *deliberately* dilapidated. That's why they introduced the sex, the drugs, and the hypnotic music to stimulate the baser instincts, because without that distraction they wouldn't have been able to keep their generational plan hidden. The conscious participants in this conspiracy are few and far between. Most people just accept some dog-eat-dog nonsense to rationalize their selfishness. An honest living would be too hard. Of course there is no Satan involved in the human expression of Satanism. It's more of an intradimensional invasion, a hostile takeover of planet earth that seeks to possess the living bodies of human beings by usurping, suppressing, or evicting the human spirit that came into incarnation. It sounds like science fiction but it's what is going on. The leaders you see on the world stage look like us — two arms, two legs, two eyes, two ears, ten fingers, and ten toes — but they're not us. I know this is hard. I know this is frightening, but if you don't hear what I'm saying we're going to lose this planet, this human life, this beautiful experience called life and being human, which, despite the lives of other races out there like the Andromedans, the Arcturians, the Sirians, and others, is one of the best experiences in the universe, an unparalleled opportunity to learn and grow. Nobody has our heart, our ability to feel, to create, to be spontaneous, to be in the moment the way we can. It's enviable. What we have failed to understand in the larger, multidimensional reality in which we live is the economy.

Have you ever considered what an economy really is? The Oxford dictionary defines it as follows:

> the relationship between production, trade and the supply of money in a particular country or region

Let's take a look at the language and its origin.

> The word economy in English is derived from the Middle French's *yconomie*, which itself derived from the Medieval Latin's *oeconomia*. The Latin word has its origin at the Ancient Greek's *oikonomia* or *oikonomos*. The word's first part oikos means *house*, and the second part nemein means *to manage*.

The economy is for the living, which, ironically, includes a portion of the dead, those who wander the earth too heavy to lift up, and other things outside the perception of our senses, but as real as rain. The living includes every born and incorporated person and organic entity, like insects and plants and too many more things to list here, but you get the idea. The economy of the twentieth and twenty-first century has been about god. That's what all superfluous economies are about in one way or another. There are only two required economies: survival and worship, the inner and the outer economy. When you merge the two into one thing you can be sure that you're in a mad materialistic cycle. Materialism is the product of abundance, which is why I call it superfluous. All you need is the body and the spirit.

It's not so much that we've forgotten about god, rather we've forgotten about the responsibility of god. We've never been more god-like in our pursuit of understanding and deconstruction of the universe. It's as though we want the power of god without the responsibility. This is a uniquely human disposition. It's a curious thing that we never merged the concept of economy with our spiritual lives. In a sense it's always been there. Karma is an energetic economy. It begins in our thoughts. We are responsible for our thoughts. What a shocking and novel idea. Of all the avatars to come in the last three-thousand years the one closest to being an economist is the Buddha. He explained a vast system of exchanges that took place between human beings and nature and beings in other dimensions. The economy of the Buddha encompassed both the living and the dead, as well as the never born. I suppose you could say that sin is a kind of an economy as well, where bankruptcy would be hell and solvency would be heaven.

Here's a true understanding of economy that has never been explicitly stated: In every state of being we find ourselves in, if that state of being takes place within a dualistic world, of which there are many beyond the physical, we're in an economy. Any world with a negative and a positive polarity has an economy. Economy is the management of energy that sustains the world. Every world that is dualistic is spinning. All of that spinning takes energy. That energy has to come from somewhere. The physical body is the tool that god gave us to gather up our energy. Our state of existence between lives is dependent on the energy we acquire while we're alive. The entire system is run on the limitless energy of god which becomes subject to the various laws of economy in the dimension it permeates. The moment that the god energy comes into a dualistic world it's allocated to something. If the allocation and the utility of the energy do not match up, degradation occurs.

The basics of economy for a natural human being are food, water, and shelter. After that we start considering the economy of the sensual body, sometimes called the astral body, which is related to our desire to procreate. Procreation is an economy in which we pay back the debt of being born. We owe a debt to life and creation for being allowed a human life. We pay back this debt by creating another human life and nurturing and raising it. This is our spiritual contract with physical life. We don't have to do this in every life. Now there might be a tendency among people to regard this as the end of economy, the physical and the procreative which incorporates the sensual. For most of the lower realms in our physical spectrum, plant, insect, and animal it is the total economy. The lower realms exist to support the human realm. The entire natural system is the support structure for the human economy.

For human beings we enter into a multidimensional economy. There is a mnemonic economy, the economy related to memory and especially our buried memory, our memory in the unconscious, our memory of ourselves as a being that has been here before. This economy is arranged before we're born. It's defined by the very circumstances that will unfold in our life and can be changed in the slightest of ways by our free will decisions, but, for the vast majority of human beings life is like a roller coaster on rails. We can't change our fate. We don't really have free will. It's an elaborate illusion. Don't get me wrong, we get to make decisions and the outcome of those decisions determines what happens next, but it all takes place in the sandbox of physical existence. This goes on for an indeterminate time until we cry out for god. It's a slow and laborious process that is ultimately accelerated when we enter relationship with our other forms and with our creator. But until that happens we live lives of misery and darkness that have us hovering just above the animal plane and in many instances worse than animals because we take the higher consciousness we have and apply it to the natural system like an animal, and atop that we have energy predation happening on the fourth dimension. Dogs get fleas. Deer in the woods get ticks. Humans get invisible entities that live on and through us, largely unknown and unseen. We get dead humans sharing a smoke with us, a drink, a wank. And then there's the non-human life that can pop in as well, extraterrestrials, extradimensionals, and intradimensionals, which was more rare until the mid twentieth century. Now it's quite common and slowly breaking into the collective consciousness as something we can talk about.

We sent a signal out like a flare in the night, and not just in the realm of our own time-space, our own solar system, our own galaxy, and our own universe, but elsewhere, out into the nether regions of parallel universes and lateral dimensions that exist at different frequencies right beside us, and indeed, right through the very space our bodies occupy. If you look at atomic structure you will see that we are largely an empty space between the particles of protons and neutrons. We basically said to everything that we're here and we're destructive and we pose a threat to everything around us. Then everything changed, including our economy, because an economy is really nothing more than a series of exchanges, and Roswell opened up new markets.

Nuclear weapons might be the stupidest thing the human race has done in a long list of stupid things. Fortunately for us, not all races in the multiverse, and in this universe, are as stupid or devoid of compassion as we seem to be most of the time. The extraterrestrial races that came into our time-space after the atomic testing had the ability to move within our timeline once they were in our time-space. We now have no idea what is real and what's not real in our past. We don't know if the ancient alien theory is correct. It's everywhere now if you're paying attention. Our gods were aliens. There is some truth to this, but a lot of it is the result of tinkering with our timeline and laying bread crumbs in our past that didn't exist before the extraterrestrials who came after the atomic testing. Think about it like a computer network. A single computer network might not know other networks exist outside of it, if it's a closed network. Now imagine a hacker or a group of hackers getting inside that network. What could they do? Almost anything. They could change documents and they could change the database. This is basically what happened after Roswell. You'd be amazed how similar an experiential realm is to a network. The physical body is the physical network and the astral plane is the transfer of data and the database is the akashic record. Do you remember when I said that most of the things that human beings do are metaphors for something that already exists? It's like that.

How much of us is universal and how much of us is species related? Is beauty a universal principle? Do all species regard beauty the same way? If that's the case then why are so many of these extraterrestrials hideously deformed? Why do they not respect what we respect in terms of beauty? Have they been able to produce a Beethoven, a Mozart, a Dostoevsky, a Shakespeare? How do they procreate? How long do their children spend with them before they are independant? What is the gestation period for an Andromedan mother? Do they get sad? Are we the only race with a heart? Are the aliens here as mentors? Are they here to trade? What is a galactic economy? One would assume that all planet born sentient beings in the universe would have everything they need to thrive on their planets just as we do or they would never be able to get to the point where they can travel in space. If they have everything they need on their planets, why are they going into space? What is it that they're trading and what is it that they're looking to get? What is galactic commerce? Why don't we know anything about alien culture?

Whatever happened as a result of the technology and experiments and nuclear deployment on Nagasaki and Hiroshima, we could all agree that our world changed after World War II. A secret world grew out of the National Security Act. Groups were formed that are unaccountable to the public. Whether they accurately report their work to congressional subcommittees is questionable as well. Rumors of technology transfers between extraterrestrial races and we human beings abound. Its popular name is the secret space program. What does this have to do with economy you might ask? All relationships pivot off of exchanges. Economy is the fundamental rule of dualistic realities. We can assume that if extraterrestrial races contacted us here on earth that they are also familiar with and living within dualistic realities, and, therefore, bound to the same rules of exchange. Even China, long referred to as the hermit kingdom before they opened up in the seventies and eighties to Western visitors and diplomacy, traded with neighbors for centuries through the silk road. Exchange is a fundamental principle.

The remaining question, if we take this speculative theory to its full limit, is what is being exchanged? If we're getting technology what are they getting? What is it that the human race has to offer races that are beyond us technologically? Do you think they like Himalayan salt? And what happens to us if we've gone into space? What does that mean for the whole terrestrial bound human race? For lack of a clearer footprint in language, what does it do to our karmic relationship with our reality? What is the new reality of exchanges we exist within? And most importantly, why is nobody telling us? Do you really think for a minute that the intelligence agencies of the world, at least in the first world — CIA, Mossad, MI6, CSIS, ASIS, DGSE — don't know what's happening at the Mother of Darkness castle? Do you really for a minute believe that the senior politicos and the senior money people in every major nation don't understand what's going on in this subculture? Do you really believe for a minute that all of the major industries that contribute to the perception of reality in the West, are not somehow involved in this subculture of Satanism and ritual sacrifice? We are living in hell. You don't have to wait till you die to go there anymore. In typical Western efficiency they've brought it to our front door, *Uber Hell*, delivered on time or free.

The final economy of man is the spiritual economy. It begins at the mnemonic body and goes all the way to the soul. The mnemonic body is that part of us that contains all the memories. These memories transcend our physical existence, extending into a realm of consciousness that we may refer to as the universal mind. When fully comprehended and integrated into our awareness, they have the potential to transform us into beings connected to the universal consciousness. Beyond this identity is god. It's almost pointless to talk about this because it has no tangible qualities or conceptual qualities or sensual qualities, although it's all of these things. These things would not exist without the spiritual identity because it's the energy source and seed form of all the other bodies which project us right into the physical world.

But basically, we can say that there are five major bodies of man and each has its own economy. The final body of man, the soul, really doesn't have an economy because it has no needs other than to be realized, but that need for realization takes place within a physical body, so we get the idea of economy. At a certain point we're going to have to allocate part of our resources to discovering who and what we are. In the present historical record this has been done by renunciates. A renunciate is a person who turns their back on the first four economies of food, water, shelter, and procreation and goes and lives in a more solitary way with minimal food and minimal material possessions in pursuit of these realizations. This is how our spiritual economy begins. No, I don't want to get into a big theological debate here about whether we live once or many times. The truth is we live many times. It's always been this way and every religion knows this. The Jews are starting to talk about it now in the rabbinical circles and they give reasons for why it was withheld for the last X number of centuries. The Christians had it taken from their teachings in the Council of Nicaea in 535 ad. Like most things in the Christian world this was deliberately done to control the population. The Muslims never had a concept of reincarnation. Everybody else on the planet has had some form of understanding of reincarnation. I bring this up in context to economy because it explains why not everybody has the need to fulfill a spiritual economy in every life and why it's only a small portion of the human race that goes off in any given generation and practices this final economy.

It used to be that the practitioners of this spiritual economy were the leaders of a society. We used to call them Shaman or medicine men. They ruled alongside a chief who was responsible for the physical survival of the tribe and the state of the tribe in conflict or warfare. In the more advanced civilizations, like our Western civilization, we turned all of this over to institutions. Our final economy, the spiritual economy, gave birth to the first institution in the Western world, the Vatican. Now, whatever you think of Jesus Christ is your business. I personally think he is one of the most remarkable people in the human record and I try my best to live by the edicts of the Gospels. The first organized spiritual economies took place in the ancient world. They were all part of sequestered and secretive institutions. We see this in Sumeria, Babylon, Egypt, and Israel, who separated their priests into various responsibilities related to the temple. Now, the irony, or inversion, of man is that most of what we call predation takes place in the dimension just beyond the physical, what we're calling in this text the sensory or sensual economy or the astral economy. This is where most of the very negative stuff is and where most of what we call energy harvesting, entity botherance, entity association, and entity possession takes place. In our arrogance we don't admit this. We bottle this entire phenomenon up in the medical science of psychiatry and enrich pharmaceutical companies that narcotize these poor people to near unconscious states. The Industrial Revolution separated our spiritual and scientific communities and in the area of consciousness this was a huge mistake.

These institutions that formed after World War II governed literally every aspect of our lives. In the Commonwealth countries — those colonies descended from Britain — we call them ministries. It's a curious language affectation coming from the original Protestant minister, which is one who ministers to people. It's worth taking a look at this word.

minister noun

> often Minister (in the UK and many other countries) a senior member of the government who is in charge of a government department or a branch of one

minister to phrasal verb

> minister to somebody / something (formal) to care for somebody, especially somebody who is sick or old, and make sure that they have everything they need

Minister was the original title for a clergyman of the Protestant religions. Protestantism evolved out of what we call the European enlightenment and commenced with the Geneva Bible and the King James Bible. Both of these Bibles went back to the original Hebrew for their creation. The Vatican favored Latin for all of its sacred texts, and when Gutenberg invented his printing press and the idea to make a Bible for the whole world came about, the Vatican was in no mood to share their language technology. After all, it was an economy that had allowed them to rule for more than a millennia. Why lift the patent and make the technology generic? This commenced the great European wars which culminated in the battle between the British Navy and the Spanish Armada, in which, miracle of miracles, the British were able to best the Spanish, which at the time, was almost inconceivable. Spain had become the war center for the Vatican. The Spanish exercised that power all through the Inquisition and the witch burnings and all the other mayhem that attended the rule of the Vatican. Now, in our modern time we look back at that as complete lunacy, a *dark age* in the history of man, but as you'll find in the body of this book, witchcraft is real, commiseration with demonic and diabolical forces to the detriment of man is real, and these forces need to be combated.

I can't say which side the Vatican was on. I suspect that it was something that straddled the middle. The Inquisition comprised both a genuine campaign against the proliferation of witchcraft, with its associated practices of child and human sacrifice, as well as a strategic effort to uphold control and authority over Europe, as sought by the Vatican. And it wasn't just Europe. The Vatican wanted the whole world under its rule. They wrote the *Doctrine of Discovery* to rationalize the usurping of the lands of the American continent from the native peoples, and they only repudiated it in the year of this writing, 2023.

The Protestant forces consolidated themselves in England with the Bank of England in 1694, and from this fiat note system, an old Babylonian magic, came the massive expansion of the British Empire as a kind of Protestant Vatican — *meet the new boss, same as the old boss.* Along with the emancipation of countries from the grip of the Vatican, came the emancipation of the Jews. European Jews were held to limited capacity in Vatican controlled countries. They were not allowed to hold public office and they were not allowed to occupy positions that required the license or authority of the church state. All that came to an end with the rise of Britain. The Jew became the new man in Europe. Protestantism had its pseudo mystics as well, like Jacob Boheme, sold to the world as a Christian mystic but really more of Kabbalah magi.

And very quickly after this, a new economy was formed which centered around prosperity and industry and expansion of empires, no different than the Vatican and in many ways even more vulgar and violent. The enlightenment was not an emancipation from the tyranny of religious dogmas, it was a transfer of power from one dogma to another, the latter bringing with it the Kabbalah and the proliferation of European secret societies centered on religious awareness. Even the Vatican itself had to adapt. They created the Jesuit order at the behest of Saint Ignatius of Loyola, and the Jesuits became a very dark arm of the Vatican involved in the secret society game. The secret societies defined the Western economy for the centuries leading us up to this point.

The twentieth century, with its Industrial Revolution and the rapid invention of technology created an atmosphere within the human race, at least in the first world, the West, where religious and spiritual values were put aside. We put our faith in sciences, the discoverer of all things, and that which would finally reveal the purpose of human life. In doing this we put aside all of our old imaginative structures and imaginative bridges that had connected us to other worlds, and we stayed firmly within this rational, black box scientific reality. We scoffed at the idea of demonic possession and put our faith in psychiatry, yet, throughout this, one religious ideal has maintained itself, presenting itself as a social justice ideal, and that is the reconstruction of the Third Temple of Solomon, which is now the site of the second holiest mosque in the Islamic world.

Some three and a half billion people on this planet are tied up in the Abrahamic religions. The Abrahamic system has twenty-eight major prophets. The last two prophets account for ninety-nine percent of the Abrahamic population, Jesus Christ and Muhammad. With the enlightenment and the proliferation of the *Geneva Bible* and the *King James Bible* another thing happened, European secret societies formed. Most of the material that formed the basis of these secret societies were aspects of the Kabbalah, given by the European Jewish community to gentiles. This magical system formed the basis of, or, at the very least, profoundly influenced Freemasonry, the Martinists, the Rosicrucians, and countless others.

We now find ourselves on the cusp of the third temple being reconstructed. The government of Benjamin Netanyahu has become more and more belligerent about this goal. It was largely due to the secret society members, and government and intelligence organizations like MI6 and the CIA, which aided the Jews in getting this far in their goal of creating the Third Temple. The temple plays a curious role in the lives of Jews because it was constructed by a king who never claimed prophet status and was never awarded prophet status in the Jewish religious system. Solomon was and always has been a sociopolitical Jewish figure, not a prophetic Jewish figure. However he brings with him the magical system given to him, or perfected by him, through his association with all of the magical systems that existed in his time, which, if you examine the artifacts of these cultures through the lens of popular writers on this topic, were given to these races by extraterrestrials, specifically the Anunnaki.

Everything is a metaphor. When you start to develop the ability to use metaphor it means that your consciousness is expanding. In the end, metaphor is nearly useless but to get closer to the end it's very useful. So let's create a metaphor here. Computers have evolved enormously in three decades. In the early nineties they were just starting to enter homes. I remember getting my degree in journalism in Toronto and graduating in 1992. We had a few Mac computers to do layout for the school newspaper but layout was still done with a ratio wheel and a pica ruler. That's how far back I go. Computers operate from coding languages. The coding language is compiled. Now, like any other language, the coding language has a foundation. These are all the things that the language can and can't do. So Java has foundation classes. C++ has foundation classes. All the major coding languages have foundation classes. The aggregation of the foundation classes are what's known as the application programmer interface or API. So computer language foundation classes would have things like cornering, you know, the corner in an application on your desktop? So if you're working on Microsoft Word, it has four corners. Any one of those four corners can be clicked on, to drag the application longer, wider or both. That's all in the foundation classes. And if you were to go and look at the C++ foundation classes you would find a corner foundation class. And it would tell you everything you can do with a corner. I use computer languages because computers have been able to create an entire world and it's done from a relatively simple API. The point I'm trying to make is that you don't need a whole lot to build an expansive reality. God didn't need a whole lot to build the universe. He just needed a consistent foundation class. We might not call them foundation classes. We might call them elements. We might call them the rules of the universe. But you get the point. Now here's the real point. What was the API that built Western society? If you said anything other than religion you would be wrong.

The API of Western civilization is Christianity. You might think we've outgrown it, but that's just not possible. The social consciousness we have now is built on top of the generations that preceded us. The foundation of our culture is embedded in us genetically at this point. The righteous soldier of Christ is now manifested as the screaming transgender activist. The actual transgenderism is not a Christian value, but the self-righteous tantrum and *standing up* for what you believe is right is definitely part of the Christian API.

I lived in Taiwan from 1992 until 1994. I graduated university in the middle of a recession. I had student loans to pay. I needed to do something, so I went over to Taiwan and became an English teacher. It was a remarkable culture to experience, so different from my birth culture. They seem to do everything in a slightly different way. They ate with chopsticks. They built toilets right into the floor so that you had to squat on your haunches. Some of the things they did were the same way as us. The clothes had buttons. The pants had legs. The most marked differences were foundational. Sometime in the first couple weeks you're in Taiwan you get a debriefing from the other English speaking immigrants living there. It usually happens in a pub. It's all the small do's and don'ts in that culture and all the things to be cautious of, and the seasoned English speaker who has been living in that culture for a number of years delivers it like a high priest talking to an acolyte. You usually have to buy them a couple beers too. The most disturbing thing I heard was if while driving around on your motorcycle — because we all drove motorcycles in Taiwan — you get hit by a car and you can still move, then you should crawl off the road. The reason was because the driver who hit you, will throw his vehicle in reverse and drive over you in a deliberate attempt to kill you. In the Taiwanese system it's cheaper to kill you and pay death benefits than it is to pay ongoing medical bills. I was aghast. I was being told that everybody in that society would do this, housewives with two children, businessmen, taxi drivers, and especially the cement truck drivers. I couldn't get my head around a society that could produce killers in this manner. I understood saving a few dollars, but taking a human life was no small matter. How could everybody do it so easily? Sure enough it proved to be true. I later read the exact same thing in the biography of a British army officer during World War II who was stationed in Hong Kong. If you get hit on a bicycle or a motorcycle, crawl off the road because they'll kill you. Not only that, if you have any kind of accident, then you're on your own. Chinese people don't involve themselves in the trouble of others. Their API doesn't have the Good Samaritan story.

Taiwan was spared the cultural revolution. It's been a largely democratic country since 1949, and before that it was run by the Japanese. All of the old Chinese culture is alive in Taiwan. It's the pure Chinese culture distilled over eight thousand years. As I thought about why somebody would drive over you to make sure you were dead, I was forced to consider the cultural API of China. It occurred to me that this was a culture built on Buddhism and Taoism. These are reincarnation teachings. In the religious apathy of the modern age, these teachings had morphed into a kind of *I'll pay for it later* attitude with everybody thinking in terms of a karmic account. Our Christian API had no such leeway. Every human life was precious and determined whether a person went to heaven or hell. In our evolution through this system we came to a higher value of an individual human life. It was all based on our foundation. The same was true of Taiwan. The generational living had embedded these precepts into the culture and into the collective consciousness.

Nobody really understands the religious texts anymore. Walk up to any Catholic priest and ask him what the holy spirit is. He'll give you a bunch of nonsense about a state of grace, or a feeling or presence, but it'll all be amorphous, nothing concrete. Anything that exists has tangible qualities. It's true that those qualities may not be material, but we live in a time where science has defined what a quark is, what antimatter is, and too many things to list here without it becoming a science textbook. If they can do it, why are the people of internal science not able to do it? Why is everything still this antiquated language coming from the belly breathers in India or the ancient Hebrews who basically stole it from all the surrounding cultures? Why can't we come up with a new language that is specific and meaningful for our spiritual lives, at least as it pertains to the foundational nouns?

We should at this stage of the game, after centuries of organized continuity within a human civilization, have a much more defined spiritual lexicon, but we don't. You might want to ask yourself why that is. Why are we still mucking about in the most amorphous of terms? Why hasn't the language of quantum mechanics and spirituality merged to give us concrete definitions of the most basic things? It may seem puritanical or trivial to you, but if we can't get the foundation right we have nothing to build upon. The foundational language is absolutely important. This book has focused on the definition of darkness. It's absolutely imperative that darkness be understood for a proper spiritual life to take place. It's absolutely imperative that the nonsensical ideas put forward by various Western religions about negative principalities and the fall of man be corrected. They have been negative since the beginning and they have been part of a negative agenda.

Religions have become the biggest play in the world. The priests and the imams and the rabbis and the yogis are all like adult supervisors at one of those indoor children's playgrounds. That is if I give them any authority at all. If you're going to make any headway in the understanding of god and creation then you're going to have to do it all on your own. It's an endless process of trial and error. But in that process, something will see you, and it will see your sincerity, and it will see your relentlessness, and it will come and aid you, but before that happens other things will come, and they will come to misdirect you. They will come to test you. There's nothing negative about this. Stop thinking in negative and positive frameworks. It's just ridiculous. There is only what is and what is not. Many of the things that are not real, can seem real. So we need a basic definition here. I have to hold myself to my own rules. The real is eternal. Anything that is not eternal is not real. This certainly fits the Buddhist definition. Let's call it the colloquial definition of Maya, which is the Buddhist term for illusion. It's not really an illusion. It's just not permanent and eternal.

The body is an instrument of darkness. It is an important instrument of darkness. It brings life. Life is light. Light is life. Absent life we cannot grow. We grow because consequence is inescapable. The system of life the body exists within assigns consequence. Everything we do is assigned to us. Everything we think is assigned to us. Our thoughts and actions are inescapable. This is a blessing.

This is how we learn.

There are three main parts of creation. There is matter. The body is matter. The body lives within an environment of matter. There is the middle kingdom. The middle kingdom is three principal worlds after matter. Each of these principal worlds has many sub worlds and realms. They are uncountable. After the middle kingdom comes spirit. Actions take place in matter. Thought and feeling take place in the middle kingdom. The world of spirit is our goal.

To achieve our goal we have to cross the middle kingdom. There are many deceptions in the middle kingdom. There are many distractions in the middle kingdom. There are many places to rest in the middle kingdom. The middle kingdom does not have the requirements of economy. It is different from the world of matter. The body demands attention. There is an energy mandate. There is a water mandate. There is a recharging mandate. We must eat food. We must drink water. We must sleep.

The body casts us into darkness. We are born to a world. We are born into a solar system. The sun illuminates our world half the time. The darkness we are cast into is separation from the middle kingdom and the world of spirit. We have connections to both of these worlds through the body but they have to be developed. The world we live in does not encourage their development. This is why it is said that the body casts us into darkness. The language of darkness is fear. In darkness we cannot see. When we cannot see we cannot move. When we cannot move we are immobilized. When we are immobilized we panic. What we cannot see is death. We can conceive of it. This is the curse of human sentience. The lesser kingdoms below us on the planet are not born under this curse. Only human beings are born under this curse.

The body is a clock. The clock measures are life. The gears of the clock are within our DNA. From the deoxyribonucleic acid the gears extend into the cells. Our cells regenerate themselves. At a certain point in our life the DNA tells the cells to stop reproducing themselves. A human life is sustained by an ongoing process of cellular cloning. Every seven years a human being is a completely new creature at a cellular level. It is because the body orchestrates and times our death that we can say it is an instrument of darkness.

The darkness propels us. If it were not for the darkness we would not move. If it were not for the fear of death we would not move. This movement is critical. We have to move all the way through the middle kingdom. It is in the middle kingdom that we take our rest between lives. These bodies come and go. This is the principle of reincarnation. You do not reincarnate. You never existed. While the body was occupied you went to sleep. You lived in darkness. You awoke in death. What are you? If you are not the body, then why do you take a body?

The body is the root system of creation. It is in the material world that we get the nutrition of god. When our belly is full we can live on the fat of that spiritual nutrition in the middle kingdom like a bear hibernating. But it is only a hibernation. It is not a permanent state. Some things stay a long time in the middle kingdom. They do this in violation of the law. Anything which violates the law of god blocks the flow of creation. It is no different than the way a hydroelectric dam blocks a river on this planet. Nothing is hidden from us. There are no mysteries. Life is constantly speaking to us. We just don't understand the language.

There are many things in the middle kingdom and they have

been there since before we recorded things on this planet. Or we might say before this cycle of recording things on this planet. The material plane and this planet in particular are extremely unstable. There are any number of things that can happen on this planet which are cyclic and have the capacity to wipe out every facet including the records of even the most advanced civilizations. It has happened with such frequency that we can say it is the norm on this planet. There have been more civilizations that have come and gone on this planet than you would believe. Many of them were more advanced than the present state of technology in which we live. It was not the same technology. There are so many scientific foundations that multiple scientific paradigms are possible. In the paradigm we live in now we have chosen fossil fuel and silicon as the foundations. The fossil fuel is our energy system. Silicon is the basis of the artificial intelligence we have created.

All the systems of technology have the same intent. It does not matter what era or age. The technology is always energy and hyper communication. Energy is required to run the machines that do the heavy work. Hyper communication is required to form the informational event horizon that will take us to a new plateau of understanding. All technology is a metaphor or an allegory for the spiritual mission given to human beings which can be done without technology. It could be said that all technology is a distraction. If you look around you you will come to the understanding that you live in a great age of distraction.

Part III

God & Me & You

Chapter 10

A Holy Place

There is no such thing as a holy place or a holy land. People who believe such things are deluded and misguided. Certain locations can have power resonances associated with them. These can be a confluence of Ley Lines, where a saint lived, or a dark practitioner. In the case of the latter, they can both leave a resonant energy, but it's an echo of the original sound, a photocopy of an original picture, not the real thing. In the case of the former, these can be formed by underground currents of water which emanate an electrical energy, which can be detected by water diviners and scientific instruments. It's a human tragedy that people can be so mentally possessed by the concept of god but completely absent god itself. Witness the crusades. Centuries of conflict over the *holy land*. It's a farce. We have a whole new generation of morons cloaked in the new age movement who take people on sacred tours of Stonehenge or the pyramids in Egypt. If these sojourns are for tourism or for anything else, like the architecture and the wonder of the place, then so be it. That's no different from someone wanting to see a Blue Morpho butterfly and taking a trip to where I live in Costa Rica. I get that, but the sad reality of these deluded pilgrims who go to holy sites and the exploitative opportunists who organize such trips, is that they will come no closer to god. If they wanted god all they had to do was stay home and maybe fast for a week and meditate in the morning, the afternoon, and the evening, and that would have brought them closer to their maker than a ridiculous trip to the holy land. Imagine god observing this. He sends a messenger to the earth to educate us, to empower us with the energy and wisdom of the divine, and the moment said messenger is gone, people are killing each other to control the physical geography where the holy one's sandal-adorned foot touched the ground. It's enough to make you vomit. Right now there's some bed and breakfast owner in Bethlehem full to capacity year round, and doubling or even tripling his prices at Easter and Christmas, so that some moron can see the place the messiah was born. It's the same thing for the Bodhi Tree in India where the Buddha attained enlightenment. God is in the place where you have your love and your being. Nowhere else. And those places are made by us, by our intentions, our energy, and our being, and the same is true for your inner life. The temple is in your forehead when the heart is clean. The universes open up and awaken us to living imagination, an inner reality which we come to realize more and more is connected to this outer reality, this timeline we are living which we call our life.

How you see the world depends on where you see it from. If you see it from an alley in New Delhi India, you might just see the immediate, which is fine — all you really need is the immediate — and maybe all the factors of the world distill to that alley, like some socio-economic version of chaos theory. Maybe you know the world is in dire trouble by lack of extra, the extra food the street vendors had so you didn't starve, the extra change the shoppers had by the mall you begged in front of some afternoons, or the extra the government had when it sent social workers and nurses out in a white van to check your health, prescribe antibiotics for infections, and dress wounds you had been scratching. You'd know when there is less. What you might not know is why. Why is there less? What has taken from the people, the society? Where did it go? Did god forget you were living in that alley on the extra?

I see the world from a unique vantage. I see it somewhat liberated from the shackles of the formerly rich West. I came to Costa Rica in 2014 with the intent of living more deliberately, like Thoreau on Walden Pond. I held the conviction that embracing a life connected to nature was the ideal way to live, anticipating that the urban centers, now resembling concentration camps, would manifest their oppressive nature even more prominently in the years ahead. Cities always become prisons. They're even built like prisons, gridded out like computer chips — if you look at them from above — and full of rules and taxes. It's no way to live. When you understand this you then ask, why do people do it? Why do they live in substandard dwellings with no space for animals and pay for everything — water, heat, electricity, parking, transportation, food, and fines — and why do they not ask themselves if there isn't something better?

One of the things which astounded me the most when I moved to the Talamanca Mountains was the color of egg yolks. When you get an egg from a chicken coop, the yolk is tangerine orange. The egg yolks back in Mississauga, the western joining municipality where I raised my son, were pale yellow. I learned that through corporate farming the hens are kept under a fluorescent light twenty-four hours a day, and that this bio-hack produces two eggs in a twenty-four-hour cycle rather than just the one nature intended. They call that *progress* in commerce. Torture the animals. Raise them in tiny cages. Squeeze two eggs out of them. Deplete the nutritional value of a single egg by fifty percent, and cut the fowl's miserable life of being caged and driven insane by at least half, but, because chickens reproduce so swiftly, there's always a steady supply of chickens to abuse, and a steady supply of consumers who don't care what their diet is doing to the chickens or that they're not really eating eggs as nature intended them to be, and that's just chickens. What corporate farming does to all the other animals is equally grim, but there's really no other way to feed a city of millions, and, because all the food has to be shipped into the cities by truck or train, then slaughtered, if not brought in on refrigerated cars already butchered. It's a horror show. People don't think about it because they don't see it.

I was a vegetarian for a decade before I moved to Costa Rica; Almost a vegan except for a little milk in my coffee from time to time. I lived close to an Indian market, and I adopted their diet of legumes, curries, and rice. I was not under any religious edict from a school or system that I was studying at the time. I just decided I didn't want to eat fish, fowl, or meat anymore. It reached a point where it disgusted me. I don't know if this was an outgrowth of the daily meditation I had been doing for a couple of decades, or whether it was a natural outgrowth of my life. I was fine being vegetarian.

When I came to the mountain I returned to meat, with one caveat — I raised and butchered the meat myself. This is something everyone who eats meat should experience. For a chicken it's quick but disturbing. One moment the bird is moving and the next it isn't. You have to boil the chicken. It makes it easier to pull the feathers, otherwise it will take hours. A pig really brings death into focus. The kill weight for a pig is one hundred kilograms. If you let them get any bigger it becomes difficult to kill them. Pork is a poor person's meat, and it has to be respected as such. They mature to harvest in just six months. Nothing in the human diet grows quite so quickly. You have to boil a fifty gallon drum of water over an open fire, then pour pots of scalding water on the dead pig. That's how you scrape off the first layer of skin and the hair. It takes a while. On the mountain a pig harvest is a community affair. There are tasks for the women, tasks for the men, and tasks for children. The pig is brought from the pen to the kill spot. We put some apples down in front of it. It gets the head in the right place and distracts the animal. Then the sledgehammer is brought down square between the eyes. This sends the pig back a step and drops it to one side. There are usually convulsions. I have never seen a pig knocked unconscious no matter how hard the sledge was swung. I was the *matador*, which, if you don't know Spanish, means *killer*. This is the job nobody wants to do. On a farm kill without a gun, a large knife is used. It has to be at least ten inches long. The knife is slipped in behind the top of the chest bones lengthwise to the pig's body and then plunged into the heart. If it's done correctly the pig is dead three seconds after the sledgehammer hits its forehead. There is very little suffering. I could get the knife in very fast. It alarmed people a little. I was asked if I had killed pigs before. I said no. Eyebrows were raised.

You can sense the moment when the animal passes. You can feel the spirit leaving. There's a little door that opens from the body to another world and the spirit leaves. Not so much with a chicken, but a pig… a pig halts you in your tracks for a second or two. You might look off into the jungle, or up into the sky. There's just a reverence. It became quite spiritual for me. I said prayers to myself, thanked god and the animal for feeding my family. I became particular about whom I would kill a pig with. Some guys on the mountain thought it was funny. These were the punks, the small-time drug dealers and thieves, people of bad character, and it was interesting to me that a pig kill would reveal their true character. Childish people laugh at death. Mature people honor it. You should be silent for a few moments after a kill. The dozen or so people helping out should be still and quiet. Some women leave for the actual kill. They walk around to the other side of the barn. They don't want to see it. This is another form of reverence. But the goof that giggles or is fascinated with the kill in a morbid way, at times I had a flash of anger, an impulse to kill them right after I killed the pig, as though death was a mental infection.

One time a friend at the foot of the mountain whose family owned a convenience store asked if I would allow his twelve-year-old son to plunge the knife. I said sure. I figured it was some rite of passage for the boy and his father. He was a fine lad and I had known him for a couple of years already. We boiled the water and prepped the kill. The hammer man was ready and passed me a knowing glance. I nodded, and we got the pig in place and placed the apples on the ground, which the pig immediately started eating. I passed my eleven-inch *Buck Hoodlum* — a two hundred dollar hunting knife I had bought before I came to Costa Rica — to the twelve-year-old boy. His whole body started to tremble and water gushed out of his eyes. I took the knife from his hand and gestured at the hammer man to hold. I walked away from the crowd by the pig and knelt down in front of the boy on one knee. He was ashamed of his trembling and his tears. I assured him it was no small thing to kill a large mammal and that his reaction was spiritually correct. I further told him that if he wanted to try again when he was older then that too was okay, and I concluded by saying that maybe he would never kill a pig, and that he should honor the heart god gave him. He was very happy with my words. We went back to the group and I killed the pig. Nobody laughed at the boy and everybody understood exactly what had happened. That twelve-year-old boy was more mature than the adult goofs who laughed at a pig kill, the same goofs I banned from my kills. The killing caught up with me after a while, after a dozen or so pigs. I started thinking about it more. I eventually found my child's heart again, just like the boy, and I couldn't do it anymore. I returned to being a vegetarian. My wife was a little upset. She had a diet like a wolf, farm raised on regular meat, but I was intractable — no more meat. If you eat meat, just once in your life you should kill a large mammal.

The house which I chose to build with my son was an earthbag house, sometimes referred to as hyperadobe. I waited until my son finished high school. He was eighteen years old. Being a father has been the greatest responsibility of my life. My son was the first person I could love with my guard down, the first person I truly shared myself with. When you grow up the way I did, and when you live a life like I did, human love is more difficult. It's not that your heart is closed, quite the opposite — my heart was tremendously moved in meditation, creative writing, powerful cinema and art, and by the suffering of others — I had a huge heart, but true vulnerability and truly letting go with another person was very difficult for me.

I was born within a family curse. People don't understand what a curse is. In the inverted way we look at everything in the world now, we believe a curse is misfortune. In fact, in the present time in which we live, those who are cursed prosper. Just look at any capital city, like the capital I was born into, Ottawa. If you were to visit it you would find it quite lovely, but, like all power centers, it has a very foul energy. That energy is like a psychic toxin that is absorbed by everyone who lives there. The longer you live there the more intoxicated you become. Because the nature of the toxin is power, it blocks the reception of love. Power and love are antipodes in our reality and cannot co-exist in the same space, like light and dark, there can only be one or the other. The positive pole is always connected to the divine, so it trumps the other. When a fire is lit in the forest it pushes back the darkness, same thing when a light is turned on in a room. The problem with power centers is they are an economy. The people in the power center support it, protect it, and nurture it.

My family fit in perfectly in Ottawa. Power masks personal defects. Power always gives you a reason to do something, even if what you're doing is evil. Nobody thinks you're evil. You're just doing your job. How could that be evil? My father was as corrupt outside the house as he was within it. He was an economist, and, though I can't prove it, I'm pretty sure in his many travels he was the last friendly face the foreign government saw before they met the *economic hit men*, made famous by the book written by John Perkins. My father did the bulk of his traveling before I was twelve-years-old. He was gone several months a year. Later, my mother started traveling with him and a grandmother would tend to us for two or three weeks. When my father came home from these travels we always got some trinket from the country he visited, a sombrero, an Indian shirt, or something you might pick up at the airport on your way out. There were always the stories, too. My father had witnessed a beheading in Saudi Arabia, the dead cart in India, which was an oxen pulled cart that would roll through streets in the morning, admonishing people to bring out their dead so they could be taken for cremation. He visited prisons in Turkey, and he went into East Germany before Glasnost. He stayed in what they called a five-star hotel in Moscow, but he had this great anecdote for why communism would fail. He said that none of the room doorknobs in the hotel were in the same place on the door, and he said that this was because the interest in doing a good job was so low they just didn't give a shit. I have to hand it to the old man, he could distill things to an almost perfect understanding. Imagine getting that insight into communism when you're fourteen-years-old.

If you live in a capital city, and you're part of the machinations of that city in the governance of a nation, then you're probably part of a family line that is in some way cursed. I know this sounds antithetical, but it's only because you don't understand what a curse really is. The fundamental nature of a curse is spiritual. Therefore, a cursed person has a more difficult time forming a relationship with the divine. God is nothing but love. The force of love as it manifests in the various planes that comprise our total multidimensional reality and permeates outwards becomes many smaller forces. This is what Lao Tzu was trying to tell us in the *Tao Te Ching*.

He tried to explain the *way* in the Taoist scriptures. It should be clear to anybody who is paying attention in their lives that the greatest figures to have come to our planet are the sages. The fact that we have not grasped this, and, worse still, that we have not begun to live more intentionally and spiritually is *prima facie* evidence that the negative principality is in control of this planet, or, to stay within my narrative and scope, the West, but given the dominance of the West over the world for the last three-hundred years, it might apply to the world, but the outlier places are not under the curse. They are free to receive the divine energy, which is the blessing in a life. Whatever that force was that greeted Christ in the desert — it controls everything now.

Do you feel cursed, as you sit in your condominium on beautiful leather furniture watching a fifty-two-inch television, chatting with your mistress on an iPhone, a half pint of Ben & Jerry's ice cream on the mahogany coffee table? The cursed never know they're cursed. It's part of the curse. What Stephen King doesn't understand about the supernatural wouldn't fit into an NFL stadium if it was empty. It's the stupid leading the stupid, and it has gotten more stupid every generation since the Second World War. It's the World Series of stupid now. This is how it all comes together. This is what they've been working on since 1947. The occult elites of this planet saw something during that wartime that set in motion a plan so diabolical that it is profane to speak about it in public, but I'm well versed in profanity, after all, I was raised on the streets from the age of sixteen. If you're succeeding in this world, you're among the cursed, because the world itself is cursed now. I can't be any more clear.

Don't get me wrong, you can have a good life if you work hard, but the work has to be honest. It can't be some bullshit job at the Ministry of Finance. But you're still subject to your consciousness, and if left unguarded you will be breached. The CIA director in 1981, William Casey, famously said *we'll know our disinformation program is complete when everything the American public believes is false.*

Why would that be the goal of the intelligence service? And why are they even operating on the domestic population? It's illegal for them to do that.

The old man's tutelage of the dark world continued. I remember one evening when I was seventeen-years-old and visiting the family for dinner. The evening news was on. I had bussed in from my rooming house in another part of Ottawa. The news was covering a story out of the Philippines. Some guy was walking across a tarmac at an airport. The front door opened, and the old man entered the house. He walked down the hallway to the family room where I sat with my brother watching the television. He greeted us both and then glanced at the television. He said to us, *do you see that guy on the tarmac*? My brother and I both nodded. The old man said, *he'll be dead in a week.* I looked curiously at my father and said, *cancer*? My father said, *no, the CIA is not done with Marcos yet.* A week later the man was shot dead on the tarmac of the Manila International Airport. That man was Benigno *Ninoy* Aquino Jr. The airport he was killed at is now named after him. He was a political opponent of Marcos and had been living in exile for several years. His return to the country represented a direct challenge to the authority of Marcos, and thereby, through the dark tutelage of the old man, the authority of the CIA. I never clarified with the old man, whether he was directly involved in briefings that stated the man was going to be killed or if it was just an affectation of his years in affairs of state. One thing was certain, it didn't bother the old man at all. He knew how the world worked, and he wasn't about to stand up in the canoe and tip it over.

This was the environment within which I was raised. I kept my distance from the family home and only visited occasionally because my mother was distraught. I found the energy of the home oppressive, like visiting a catacomb that was demonically possessed. My mother and father were like obsidian stones to me, pure black and impenetrable. All my hope and happiness disappeared when I was around them. I don't think they realized how dark they had become. My mother had never properly dealt with the suicide of her father, and my father was demonically oppressed, though it would take me decades more to figure this out, to crystallize it within me, though, truth be told, I always knew. The soul knows things for which it has no words. It was around this time, the Philippines assassination of Aquino, that I found meditation and began the long journey to my becoming.

There's something very liberating about being unmoored from family obligations. When my father kicked me out I was the free agent I always wanted to be since the age of four. I suspect they thought it was going to break me in some way, but it had the opposite effect. I became much more diligent outside the home. I found construction jobs to work in the summer to bank a little money. It was brutal work but I needed the money. In the winter times I worked in restaurants. When I was under nineteen years of age I worked as a busboy or a dishwasher and after nineteen I started working as a waiter or a server. These two basic trades, construction and the restaurant industry, would serve me well for ten years. I maintained a cordial relationship with my family as an independent person. I visited once in a while when I was still in Ottawa, but the urge to go out and explore was very strong. I finished my high school equivalency at Algonquin College in Ottawa.

For most of my life in Canada, from the moment I left my father's house under police escort, I lived on the lowest rung of society. I was like what they call the *untouchables* in India. I lived in rooming houses, welfare hotels, and in the worst neighborhoods. I got to know the streets like Martin Scorsese. I knew whores and killers and drug dealers and money lenders and enforcers for various criminal organizations. That's the power structure on the street. It's similar to the power structure of officialdom, the power structure of a capital city like Ottawa, but the difference is everything follows natural law on the street. The position of the king is always subject to being usurped by a contestant. All contests are by combat. When a leader at the top of a criminal organization is going to be replaced, he's killed. As far as I'm concerned, this is completely natural, and we as citizens should not interfere with it. It's absurd that we charge these people with murder and put them in prison. It doesn't change or halt the growth of crime in a society in any way. Yet we do it. And why do we do it? We do it for the sentimental and cursed view of reality held by all the minions who work in officialdom. We don't want to offend their sensibilities. Murder must be punished. This is true, but at the level of the street it is always punished, and in a much more efficient way and in a way that doesn't cost the taxpayers anything. It's a basic understanding in the lawless world and every single person in a criminal organization understands this. The irony of the lawless world is that there's actually more law. The lowest position you can hold in the criminal world, aside from somebody who harms women and children, is that of a snitch, a rat, an informer. This means you turned your back on the law of the lawless world, and you went into the regulations and the policies and the statutes to find salvation. In the criminal world this is correctly perceived as selling your soul to the devil. It's amazing how many things they get right. You should die by the law under which you lived. Anything else is bad for your soul. Indecision is bad in the afterlife.

My son and I spent a lot of time together. When I lived in Canada I never worked full time. I worked contracts. This was how the high technology market worked from the late nineties onward. I made a point of being off for the summers. His mother worked an office job in the insurance industry. I made myself available for daycare. He would get dropped off in the morning and then picked up again at six in the evening. We formed a very strong bond in the years from about eight-years-old to thirteen. I taught my son how to meditate, and he took to it right away. He started doing it on his own. We had a very powerful experience the first time we meditated together. The sitting was about an hour. I was astounded that he could do it. When we finished he told me something he had been sitting on for a year. His best friend, Noah, died of leukemia the year before. It was a long and painful battle that went on for three years. His teachers went to his house in the evening to teach him when he couldn't go to school in the first grade. They didn't want him to fall behind a year and lose his friends, of which my son was his best. It looked like Noah was going to make it. He showed up in September to start the second grade, but shortly into the first semester the cancer came back. He was gone by the spring. The funeral was one of the most brutal things I have ever had to attend. There were no children, just the parents of the children who knew Noah, his teachers and the vice-principal of the school, and friends and family of Noah's mother and father.

After the meditation my son said he had something to tell me. He told me that Noah had been coming to him every night when he went to sleep. I asked him why he was just telling me then, as

Noah had been passed for a year. He shrugged his shoulders, which is the universal child language for he knew, but he didn't have the language to explain himself. The answer came to me because we had just finished meditating. That's the way it works for me. I don't know, then I know. It defines god for me, knowing, and often with no rational explanation for how I know. Remember that kid in high school math who could walk up to the board and write the correct answer every time? That's god for me. The teacher who asks me to show my work, or I'm going to fail or get a lower mark is the devil, is Ottawa, is jealousy and futility. If I don't know something it's because I'm not supposed to know. I don't get resentful. I don't try to crack it with some psychic power, astrology, or any other such nonsense. Psychic and spiritual are two totally different things, but in the spiritually emaciated world in which we now live, few people understand that. I told my son that Noah was worried about him. I told him that night, when Noah came to him, to tell Noah that he was okay, and that Noah could move forward on the other side. My son did as I told him and Noah never came back after that. It was an incredible spiritual insight for him and for me, a tying off between the visible and the invisible, the living and the dead.

When he was thirteen-years-old my son and I went to India for a month. We landed at Indira Gandhi Airport and began an adventure. We rode the poor car of the train all over Punjab Province, woke to goats licking us or chickens in cages. It was wild. These Gypsy hermaphrodites would get on and shake everyone down for money, whatever spare change the poorest of the poor had. You could travel four-hundred kilometers for less than five dollars. We saw the Golden Temple of the Sikhs, stayed in cheap hotels, and visited ashrams. We had been meditating together for five years by that point, one-hour sessions. Brandon knew the basics of internal gazing, the power of syllables and especially vowels, and his tying together of the invisible and the visible had progressed well.

Our next big experience together was working on the Costa Rica house project. It was originally designed to be a year off for my son, a respite from any committed life like college or university, or even trade apprenticeship like plumbing or electrical. I was working at a large Canadian bank as a technical writer in their technology department. They thought I was in Canada. I was allowed to work remotely, but Central America was not part of their definition of remote. There were times I would be in a conference call with a half dozen engineers and my boss, and a rooster would sound off in the background, and this happened in the middle of January when my colleagues were in sub-zero temperatures. I had to think on my feet. If somebody said, *did I just hear a rooster*? I would say something like, *yes, that's the message signal on my Samsung phone*. I'm pretty sure my boss figured it out in the second year. There were project managers I worked with on subprojects who were aware of my situation, and I became something of a folk hero amongst a certain group at the bank. My brother had worked at the same bank for twenty-five years and crawled his way up the ladder to vice president. He was a workhorse. A seventy-hour week was the norm for him and that went on for a couple of decades. By the time I was working at the bank he had already moved on to the Canada Pension Plan, from which he retired second in command. My brother lives the curse. He's a remarkable fellow in many ways, but there's really no *him* to speak of. He has no favorite writer. He has no favorite book. He has no favorite musical artist. He has no favorite music album. To the best of my knowledge he has no favorite song. He has no favorite director. He has no favorite genre of cinema. He has no favorite movie. He works and he golfs.

All my life I was beset by foul spirits from time to time, a darkness if you will, and I concluded that it was *in the blood.* I had watched my father struggle with these same dark forces all my life. Interesting that we have that general understanding, that general language — *in the blood.* I didn't grant very much access to my son for my parents. You might find that cold, but given what I have already told you in this story, and given what I am now telling you — that I became aware through my spiritual practice of a foul spirit in my family — and I simply did not want my son infected with it. I localized my mother and father as the main carriers of this spiritual infection. They circumvented me from time to time through my brother and through my ex-wife, my son's mother, but for the most part, it was an effective embargo. Because my father was an economist, and because I picked up a lot about economics at the dinner table, the topic somehow merged with my spiritual life. Economics and spirituality are the same thing when you understand both correctly. We are given a life measured in breaths and heartbeats, the metronome of a human existence, and we are given a spiritual dowry, a connection with the divine energy which begins to recede around the age of eight, not by any natural cycle, but more by the inclinations of our societal structure. We have god when we are little children because it is natural. The human form was created to grow into god. This is why Christ said, *Except ye be converted, and become as little children, ye shall not enter into the kingdom of heaven,* and this is why the Satanists and psychopaths, described to us by Carine Hutsebaut, torture and destroy children. It's a war against self in the case of the psychopath and a war against god in the case of the Satanist, and both are angry and petulant.

The labor of building the home in the Talamanca Mountains was the anecdote to my malformed relationship with my own father. I spent a total of two years, on and off, working and finalizing the project with my son. In the process he learned to speak Spanish fluently. He brought a friend with him for six months, a boy he had known since kindergarten, a boy who had also known Noah, and they worked on the mountain while I worked my job remotely from a rented house at the base of the mountain. We went through all the lessons of living and building in Costa Rica together. We grew closer. We continued to meditate together when time permitted. I watched him crew ten men and earn their respect by his ability to work alongside them under the grueling sun near the equator. There were no professional construction people on the project. I only hired the campesinos from the mountain, dirt farmers and their sons. Earthbag building is not complicated. It requires only attention to line, form of the bags, and staggering like bricks. Every coursing of bags gets two lines of four-inch barbed wire placed atop it. This gives the walls a grip and stability. As the weight of the successive lines of bags get placed down the barbed wire gets pushed into the bags. You also have to drive quarter-inch rebar through the bags in one meter lengths. This gives the walls even more tensile strength. At the top of walls you pour concrete in forms and put rebar through it into the bags below it. You build your roof on top of the concrete form. We built our window and door frames out of wood cut from the rainforest. We built into our design of the front and back buildings over two thousand square feet of roofed patio space. When the project was completed my son returned to Canada and entered into the construction trade.

I lived for a year by myself on the mountain. At that time I had two dogs and nineteen cats. My internet connection was spotty at best, and obtained through a cell phone hotspot. I looked for remote work. It wasn't as readily available as it is now, years later. Covid changed everything. I didn't need much to live, maybe four hundred dollars a month. I took up meditation at a nearly monastic level. I ate one meal of rice and beans a day, a little salt and nothing else for flavor. My life was right out of a Dostoevsky novel minus the crushing moral quandaries and intense internal suffering. I had almost nothing and I had never been happier.

It was scary at night. I'm seven kilometers into the jungle by way of a winding dirt road so potholed only a four by four could get up. You hear things at night, and the mountain gets very still. There are poisonous snakes everywhere, huge toads, and bullet ants that can leave you in crippling pain if you get bit. The part of Costa Rica in which I live is the center of narcotrafficking. The murder rate per capita makes the worst parts of Chicago seem safe, but most of that is off the mountain. The big bosses in the business buy farms, and my mountain has seen two denizens have international DEA warrants issued for them, a rare honor in the world of narcotrafficking, but as frightening to them as portrayed in *Narcos* on Netflix. The narcos loan all their stuff. I borrowed a tractor to haul some hardwood out of the forest when I was doing a new drop ceiling. I've kept renovating as I've lived here. My son and I have plans to start a small tourism business with the natives and horseback day trips there and back.

I got to know some natives from the reserve. They'd walk past my land and house on their way down to town, which was twelve kilometers from the reserve, all of it steep and inclined. The Cabecare

are incredible walkers, even their elderly can walk all day. They live the old way, no electricity, no television or radio, no plumbing, and no running water except the Barbillia River. They tell me their graveyard, which is composed of smooth round stones about the size of a soccer ball, has perhaps two hundred generations. They were living the same way in Central America when the Pharaohs ran Egypt, when Christ gave his sermon on the mount. Their matriarch is of unknown age. She was born before official record keeping began. My father-in-law, who passed away several years back at eighty-seven, told me she was already a grandmother when he came to the mountain as the first non-native in 1947. Some people peg her at one-hundred and thirty years of age. When I first met her she was walking up a steep incline on the reserve with a small hardwood log over her shoulder. My wife told me that when she was a girl and walking back up the mountain road from high school, she would sometimes find herself behind the old woman at the beginning of the journey, but the old woman would gain five-hundred meters when she went unseen around a corner on the mountain road, until she disappeared. People are convinced she's magical.

My wife was born on the mountain, in the middle of a brood of eleven children. She's the heart of the family, and all the nieces and nephews are as close to her as their mothers. She walked over to my house one day and introduced herself. I spoke my broken Spanish, and she laughed, but I was sold the first visit. The next time I saw her father at the store at the base of the mountain, on highway thirty-two, I asked his permission to see her romantically. He was impressed with the respect, and he gave his consent. Rosemary and I have been together five years now.

Every day I wake up to the sound of birdsong, the wind through the trees, and, at five o'clock in the afternoon, a large flock of green birds flies past to nest in the trees when the sun goes down at five-thirty. When it rains, dozens and dozens of frogs croak. It's so loud it can be heard through a telephone. At night the sky lights up with a dry silent lightning. People tell me it's an affectation of the electricity around a volcano that can be seen from one side of my house. It's an extraordinary night light phenomenon, on par with the northern lights in Canada. I live in a home I built with my son in the rainforest. We consecrated it with our hopes and dreams, built to our capability, so we live within our own design, and I worship god every day in this simple earthbag home we built. I don't visit holy sites, I created one.

Chapter 11

Three Books Three Schools

After several years on the mountain, comfortably married, and with many nieces and nephews around me, I decided to return to writing. My writing evolved alongside my spiritual life. My early instructors in meditation told me to keep a journal of what I saw and experienced in meditation and what I remembered from my dreams. This is how I began the habit of writing on a daily basis at eighteen years of age. It's quite amazing how any real life is built around daily habits. Even the rich people who write those crass books about becoming successful — whatever the hell that means — stress daily habits.

When I was living in the west end of Toronto, I went through an intense reading phase in the first few years. I saw so much beauty in the poets and the literature that I encountered. It seemed to me that the arts and creative writing could be an adjunct to a spiritual life, a way of bringing the energy to the earth, the way a lightning rod calls the storm's electricity. I started to practice with a lot of short stories. Expressing creativity is an exceptional means of highlighting the divine essence within you, as it embodies the role of a creator and shines brightest when humans engage in the act of creation. This is why the negative force prefers destruction. This is why the Satanists make an art form out of sacrifice and desecration. It's a mockery of the divine practice of creativity. Everything they do is a mockery and mimicry of the divine. Even their latest effort, transhumanism, is their attempt to mock the immortality given to each individual in the spiritual state. Immortality in the physical state would be lunacy. We are not meant to live thousands of years. At least not in the state in which the world exists today. In other periods throughout the cycles we do get longer lives, but that's because there's a lot more spiritual energy on the physical plane. Our collective karma makes the world darker and darker. This is what's going on in the world now. This is why there's so much darkness in the world now. We're coming to a point in time when the balance sheet must be reconciled. How the creator does that is anybody's guess.

I find thinking about these large and worldly problems to be futile, and I find people who become voices in this space to be a little ridiculous. This has been a characteristic of the human race since the prophetic lineage began in the West. I never quite understood why prophecy was a tool to demonstrate the power of the creator. All the negative principalities above us can see the future as well. Being shown the future has no guarantee that you are dealing with a positive being. How does it prove anything? We're in a horrible state of spiritual misinformation and confusion now. Everybody is running around like a chicken with its head cut off. The most basic understanding of even the first dimension above us has been lost, where that small reality had always been given to us through shamans. Now millions of people are under the influence of psychiatric counsel and powerful pharmaceuticals that further pollute consciousness and weaken the barriers around the body for demonic incursion. This was all part of the design of the twentieth century. It's not an accident. It absolutely must be understood that the demonic world is real, and the negative principalities are real, and the fact that they have human agency on this planet is real, and the fact that this human agency is controlling many of the institutions of the world now is absolutely real.

In a free will world we have no right to say that people are not allowed to worship negative deities and negative principalities. If the option to do so exists, it means god allows it to exist, and we are not to question the rules and the reality in which god creates our timelines. We are, however, allowed to question how and why so many of these demonic principalities in human form have ascended to institutional power. It is a violation of our free will right to know that they don't openly tell us that they commiserate with demonic forces, though, if you understand their symbolic legalese, they are putting out a version of fine print disclosure, usually sideways through fiction or film, but, believe it or not, that counts too. They stand before the creator and say, *we told them, and they did not dissent, so we presumed consent*, but when all of that happens within the context of an education system which is deliberately created to dim perception, a chemical diet, heavy metals sprayed in the air, a corn syrup diabetes epidemic, atheism, secularism, and Satanism, can you really say the human free will in the collective was respected? I assume the causal plane has a class of being similar, perhaps even a prototype, of what we call a lawyer here on the earth, and it's their job to argue this for our souls and incarnation credits. By the way, of the three aforementioned classes of people —

atheists, secularists, and Satanists — I would prefer to have a coffee with a Satanist. At least they're in the multidimensional game. Atheism is the highest declaration of ignorance a human being can make — there's really no overstating the stupidity of it. I don't dispute the right to disagree with the definition of god, but the notion that consciousness is purely biological and ends with the body is my point of contention. Richard Dawkins is either demonic or an idiot. There's not much wiggle room.

I wasn't sure what kind of writing I wanted to do. No such thing as literary fiction exists anymore. I think the last real writer we had in the English language was Cormac McCarthy. All of what we call literature now reads to me like some form of victim impact statement, somebody whines about the great injustices done to them in their lives because of their economic state or their racial identity or their gender, the guilty grants boards throw some public money at them to write their next horrible tome, and the awards committees line up to heap accolades on the poor soul, monetizing their victimhood and increasing the likelihood of their suicide. To be clear, there is no such thing as a victim in this world. Anyone claiming victim status is an idiot or a deceiver. The life I experienced at the hands of my mother and father was ordained. I chose it before I came into this lifetime. I knew what I would have to go through with this family. I chose to do it anyway. I was raised within a very strong negative environment. My parents didn't worship demonic forces. They worshiped at the Catholic church, but when you scratch the surface a little you have to ask yourself what the difference is. A cursory look at the Jesuit oath will reveal a very demonic substratum to the Catholic church.

> I furthermore promise and declare that I will, when op-

> portunity present, make and wage relentless war, secretly or openly, against all heretics, Protestants and Liberals, as I am directed to do, to extirpate and exterminate them from the face of the whole earth; and that I will spare neither age, sex or condition; and that I will hang, waste, boil, flay, strangle and bury alive these infamous heretics, rip up the stomachs and wombs of their women and crush their infants' heads against the walls, in order to annihilate forever their execrable race. That when the same cannot be done openly, I will secretly use the poisoned cup, the strangulating cord, the steel of the poniard or the leaden bullet, regardless of the honor, rank, dignity, or authority of the person or persons, whatever may be their condition in life, either public or private, as I at any time may be directed so to do by any agent of the Pope or Superior of the Brotherhood of the Holy Faith, of the Society of Jesus.

My mother flogged herself nightly in the Carmelite convent in Kingston, Ontario. The faith is insane, but I needed to realize that. People make a big deal of past lives in the new age circles. It's usually about ego and self-importance. I was so-and-so in a past life. I'm so fucking special. The work you have to do in your life is etched into the details of your life. I was born into a strict Catholic patriarchy governed by an alcoholic with a damaged liver and a hair trigger temper, a man so incapable of self-governance he nearly choked two Saturdays a month — steak night in the MacDonald home — because he refused to take smaller bites with his false teeth. I kid you not. This went on for years in my house. It got so comical I used to burst out laughing while my mother performed the Heimlich maneuver and the old man spat a chunk of near raw red meat across the kitchen, a piece of meat a Pitbull would find challenging in one bite. You can't even make this kind of stuff up. I dare you to even try. My grandparents were Protestant men who married Catholic women and practiced what one can only assume was hate-sex their whole lives. I was born on July twelve, the same day as Thoreau of Walden Pond fame, and I now live in a small and simple house I built myself, secluded in nature. My birthday is also an inglorious day in the ongoing battle between the Catholics and the Protestants, Orangemen's Day to celebrate the Battle of Boyne in which King William of Orange, a Protestant proxy for the throne of England, financed by Jews out of Amsterdam, in a bid to gain the Bank of England charter against the Catholic King James II in 1688. I can almost smell the blood from that battlefield when I think about it. It's no wonder I chose the Eastern system of meditation and contemplation in this lifetime. Who knows how many lives I spun around in Catholic and Protestant enmity.

As near as I can figure there are three schools of consciousness on the planet now. We have the Western Abrahamic systems into which I was born, and, if my reading of my life details is correct, into which I have been incarnating for some time in blood and glory. The other school is the Eastern system, the system of internal development through contemplation and meditation and mantra and spiritual exercises focused on the development of an individual human consciousness with little or no regard for the machinations of society and the laws that govern it. I was born to the Western system and migrated to the Eastern. I didn't even know about the third school until 2019. The third school is the gray zone I discovered in the three books I wrote beginning in 2019.

In 2012, I had been approached by a friend to write a book with John Edmonds on a place called Stardust Ranch. The middleman was a contemplative friend of mine I had known in meditation circles. He had become quite interested in the UFO world and had made inroads with John Edmonds. The two of them spoke quite regularly. My friend informed me that John Edmonds had killed gray aliens and that this was a story unlike any I'd ever heard before. My friend knew that all of my writing efforts up to that point in life had been concentrated in adult literary fiction. He also knew that I had a journalism degree from one of the best universities in North America. I listened to his sales pitch and originally turned him down. He kept pressing, but eventually I relented and took a Skype call with John Edmonds.

The moment I met John I was hooked. He had a folksy way about him, a kind of rancher's disposition, and he was a master orator and storyteller. I was sent pictures of dead animals on his ranch. Many of them had been killed in ways that defied logic. I saw a picture of a horse that was completely flat. The horse actually looked like a rug. All the innards and viscera and bones were missing. John told me he woke up, and the horse was in this state. I couldn't even imagine what could do that to an animal. After several introductory phone calls with John Edmonds over the course of four hours of conversation, I decided that I would take on the book project.

Let me tell you a bit about writing. When you start a book, no matter what kind of book it is, you have to finish the book. They are kind of like exorcisms. Once you begin you have to finish, or you're going to have bad luck for the rest of your life. This was no small thing for me to go into the world of UFOs as a writer. I was not a

UFO guy. I did not watch *Ancient Aliens* or any of the other crap on the History Channel related to the UFO world. I myself had had two UFO encounters. One was a classic disc that looked just like the disc from *The Bugs Bunny* cartoon. My brother and I saw it coming back from the family cottage in a place called Constance Bay just outside of Ottawa. It was hovering between some trees. I was eight years old, and my brother was nine. We were looking out the back window of a Volkswagen Bug, our knees on the back seat and our elbows up on the back ledge, our chins resting in our cupped hands. Seat belts weren't a huge deal in 1973. My brother and I made eye contact, and we said nothing. Kids instinctively know they have access to things that adults would not understand, and they keep it to themselves. I would have forgotten all about that encounter if it were not for a Christmas in the late eighties when I was home in Ottawa from Toronto. I walked through the front door with my luggage after getting a taxi from the train station. The family was already at the dining room table and there was a conversation going on. My brother was red-faced and a little livid. He turned to me as soon as I was in eyesight, and he said, *Bruce, tell everyone about the UFO we saw in Constance Bay*. I looked at my mother and my father and my sister, and they all had these stupid grins on their faces like they had been roasting my brother, who you may have understood through this story already was no paragon of imagination or open-mindedness. How he had broached the topic of the UFO and Constance Bay was anybody's guess. I immediately remembered what he was talking about and described it, and it was a one-to-one match for what he had described to those seated at the dining room table before I arrived. Everyone went quiet and reflective and the topic was changed very quickly, but not before my brother got his final dig in, which was something like, *I fucking told you*. Profanity was standard discourse in my family.

My other encounter with a UFO happened in 2002. I took twelve weeks to myself and rented a cabin in the woods of Northern Ontario. It had no electricity except for a one-hundred-meter extension cord I dragged across from the main cottage. I was working on a novel for which I needed to do a rewrite. I had to leave my rented house because I lived with two stand-up comedians and my girlfriend, after my divorce from my son's mother. It was too crowded and distracting for me to stay home and concentrate on my writing. I had secured a literary agent, and I had a real shot at a two book deal, but I needed to do some rewriting. My life dream was to be a literary writer from the moment I began keeping a dream and meditation journal. I had already entered the workforce as a technical writer and to have my dream dangled in front of me again after the devastating emotional loss of my family and the divorce was more than I could resist. I went at it the way Mike Tyson would train for a fight. The cabin was owned by a friend of mine's father. It was perfect for what I wanted to do. I stopped by a grocery store and bought several liters of maple syrup and a box of lemons. I was planning on a long liquid fast of one meal a day, two fried eggs, two pieces of dry Brown toast, and two tomato slices. The rest of my diet was just the beverage of maple syrup, water and lemon with a bit of cayenne pepper. It was an intestinal cleanse and I wanted to make sure that I was clear for the rewrite. For twelve weeks I existed with no radio and no television and no internet and I simply focused on my book. I had taken a bunch of classic literature and a bunch of books on scripture from various religions to occupy my time when I was not writing. It was also the first time in my life in which I meditated more than three hours a day. The total effect on me was staggering. After twelve weeks the manuscript was finished, and I felt illuminated, as though I was walking an inch off the ground. I was giving off some kind of crazy energy. People could pick up on it. Everywhere I went people stared at me, and they didn't even know why. This is the power of spiritual energy.

My energy started to ground the moment I got back to the four-bedroom house near my son in Mississauga. The second day back at home, I was leaving to go out and get a coffee with one of my roommates, a surly headline comedian who had never made it big but had been a contender for over twenty years. As we stepped out the front door in Mississauga we saw two lights above us that disappeared immediately by streaking across the sky. We looked at each other dumbfounded. I imagine it was the same way my brother and I looked at each other in the back of the Volkswagen bug in the early seventies. But we weren't kids, so we talked it out. *What the hell was that,* was the general question. We did what all adult minds do — we tried to rationalize it. My best guess was that it was two spotlights pointed up at the sky and that the spotlight tripod had been moved rapidly on the ground. We quickly disproved the physics of that and could come up with no other idea. I lived fairly close to the airport in Mississauga, so we hypothesized that it was perhaps some form of aircraft. That didn't make much sense either. Finally, we arrived at the obvious. It was an unidentified flying object. This was the second one I had seen in my life, both instances with witnesses, and both witnesses not readily open to flights of fancy, not easily willing to entertain things outside the rational.

Nothing prepared me for what I was going to experience writing Stardust Ranch. Just talking to John Edmonds on a daily basis was like a paranormal magnet in your life. That coupled with the concentration energy of writing and the vortex that it creates brought an energy into my life in the West End of Toronto that ended up unbalancing me. I got spooked and left the book. It was John Edmonds who came to my mind in 2019 when I decided to get back to writing. Throughout most of 2018 and the first half of 2019 I had been meditating about four hours a day. As you can well imagine, this is highly uncommon outside a monastic existence, but really what my son and I built with earthbags and wood from the rainforest was our own personal monastery. My wife spent a good portion of every day over at her mother's house with her brothers and sisters and nieces and nephews and I had a lot of time alone. I didn't put it together in 2019, but I had gone as deeply into meditation as I had on the twelve-week retreat in Northern Ontario. It's amazing to me that I didn't put together the excessive paranormal activity and the abundant meditation. So much for mindfulness; I was a contemplative idiot.

When I reached out to John in June 2019, he was quite surprised to hear from me. We stopped talking in 2012 except for a few emails. What do you say to somebody who said they would write a book on your ranch and then quit? I asked him if anybody else had attempted the book. He said *there had been several attempts and everybody had quit halfway through for reasons similar to mine in 2012.* I told him I wanted to write the book again. We both searched for the one-hundred and twenty pages we'd done on the first draft in 2012, but neither of us could find it on any of our cloud drives or any of our usual storage spaces. It's like it just disappeared. I'm like a pack rat for this sort of thing, and with twenty-five years of technical writing under my belt you could say that I'm something of an expert with technology, but no luck. The manuscript we'd started in 2012 was gone, as if it had flown over the Bermuda Triangle.

The first person to whom I'd ever said aloud that I wanted to go to Costa Rica and build an earthbag house was John Edmonds in 2012. Back then it was a fanciful dream. John had a good sense of what the future was going to bring for North America even though nobody could see it back then. John was an extraordinary consciousness and was capable of many acts of prescience and insight. When he asked me in our initial conversation in 2019 what I was doing, I told him I was living in the earthbag house in Costa Rica that I said I was going to build in 2012. He was impressed, and John was not an easy man to surprise or impress.

The second writing of the book in 2019 was a lightning rod for the paranormal. I'm amazed that my wife was able to go through this. The people I live with on the mountain are very attuned to the fourth dimension. There's a lot of lore up here in the rainforest. They have other races of beings that are not human, similar to gnomes, and flying monkeys with red eyes, and that's just the campesino farmers. The natives have a complete mythology that goes back millennia with all kinds of non-physical beings. In a way, I picked a perfect place to work on this book. In the course of writing the book, a portal started opening inside the house. It smelled like blood and copper. Sometimes things would come through the portal, invisible, but you knew they were there because they could move things around, even heavy pieces of furniture. Very early on in the second writing of the book in 2019, I was considering quitting again. The phenomenon can be quite intense, and if you're not prepared it can be quite distracting and off-putting. However, this time around, something truly extraordinary happened. My wife and I woke up on a Saturday morning and there was a ball of white light hanging from our ceiling. My wife snapped a photo of it. It hung around for about ten minutes. It had no problem being seen by us and was in no rush to leave. It had a warm and loving presence. My wife refers to it as an angel to this day. Whatever it was, it cleaned out the earthbag house and all the area around me so that I could finish the book. I don't think I would have been able to finish the book without this supernatural assistance. You'll find as you're dealing with spiritual matters, including extremely negative entities, you're not going to be able to get by without, as the Beatles said, *a little help from your friends*.

I finished the book with John Edmonds, and we published it on December 31st of 2019. It has become a bit of a cult classic in the genre. With the writing bug back upon me, and with many questions asked but not answered from the book with John Edmonds, I began to look for my next project. It emerged in the form of Robert Wiegand. Bob is nearly impossible to describe. I have never met anyone like him nor will I ever meet anyone like him again. He is a true shadow walker. He can go into other worlds, and he has the same apprehension, clarity, and perception that most of us have when we're in our physical bodies. I know maybe ten percent of his past. The rest, quite frankly, I don't want to know. He was a Navy SEAL and a former contractor for various intelligence agencies. Bob destroys the notion of a left hand or a right hand on the path back to consciousness. The book we ended up writing together was called *The Light of Darkness: A Warrior's Tale for our Time*.

This book was unbelievably difficult to write. I was assaulted by all kinds of imagery in the dream space. There was a sense of dread and depression around me the entire time I worked on the book, which was about six months. My wife reported giant beings of fourteen feet and bigger walking around the house in the middle of the night. My wife can see things that I cannot at times. As I said, she's very attuned to the fourth dimension, what we call the astral plane, as are most simple and earth-based people who live by natural law. It is a testament to how deformed our way of living in the first world has become, that we have lost this birthright connection to the fourth dimension that almost all human beings have regardless of education or position in society.

The major metaphysical aspect of this book is that there is no such thing as pure darkness. All darkness has a light woven into it that you can tune into to illuminate the darkness. This was proven out to me by Bob. The only other people I've heard talking about this on the planet are the rabbis. Perhaps there's some mention of it in the literature of the Aghoris in India, but I haven't done enough reading in the area. In the writing of this book I went into a dark world. I was there for seventy-two hours. It's very difficult to describe to people because it had no discernible phenomenon. In fact, the most descriptive thing I can say about this dark world is that it had no thoughts, no feelings, no sights, no colors, no sounds, no smells, no tactile sensibilities, and no tastes or memories. It was a place where you knew you existed, but no evidence of that existence is given. There is a strange and calming beauty to the place. For the first while I was terrified but even my own fear could not well up as an expression because this dimension had no expressions permitted. I remember coming out of it after three days and having an incredible sense of power. I knew things I didn't know before I went into that dark world. When I looked at the world around me and all its details, I could see things I had never seen before, as though the darkness had brought them into my consciousness. I was no longer afraid of evil or the demonic realm or anything of that character after these seventy-two hours in the dark world. It was a very seductive place. There was no good or bad there. This was the world of darkness. I had experienced it and been initiated into it. What I did with that initiation was up to me. I know that there are many other people on the planet with this initiation. Some of them use it in very negative ways. This is part of the initiate strata in the world described to us in Belgium by Carine Hustebaut, and around the world of the Satanic sacrifice of children. It is this darkness that allows people to participate in these rituals and conduct these rituals without being destroyed. However, over the years as I assimilated the experience of that dark world I have become aware of the fact that the darkness itself does not condone dark actions by human beings.

This is the third school on the planet. It's pure power, the antipode of love, and all four of the horsemen of the apocalypse at the same time. There is no end time prophecy. It's a plan, a drama, a theater put on by miscreants so drunk on power they're not even human anymore, so cross-influenced by negative beings that they're not even human anymore. Initiation into this third school is facilitated by rituals which consecrate the forfeiture of your humanity, and have you cross a line that you cannot uncross. It is the ultimate crossing, where all minor crossings are just rehearsals. Their numbers on the planet now are legion, and if they themselves are not actually running the countries then their controlled agents are. I'll leave you to draw up your own list. It shouldn't be hard with the information given in this book, just look for the leaders deliberately destroying their own countries, collapsing their currencies, pursuing mad flights of liberalism so antithetical to common sense and the continuity of a society they are demonic. It's not hard at all.

The third school goes back into antiquity. It has had many names. William Cooper called it *Mystery Babylon*. It has existed for centuries in the West. You can see flashes of it in John Dee and his Enochian magic, which came from the Book of Enoch. After the Bank of England formed, Freemasons started being recruited in the United Kingdom. The Rosicrucians are another variety, as are the Martinists from France. Portugal and Spain have their variety of it. They are everywhere now. The Freemasons run the drug cartels in Latin America — order out of chaos. It is the spread of dark Judaic theology through a land once dominated by a dark force, the Vatican, indeed a force that may have, through its unholy hold on power, necessitated the rise of this third school. This dark and hidden anti-yoga, practiced by power hungry neophytes, necessitated it in the same way we were led to believe we needed the atomic bomb, and then thermonuclear bombs, and then mind controlled populations through television and music and news so corrupt it doesn't meet the dictionary definition of information, and then identification chips, and then digital currency — the final coup of those same generational forces that won the Bank of England — and then we are officially the chattel of some demonic, off-world entities. Nice job humanity.

This third school has permeated our sciences and our intelligence agencies. It has created spin-off programs like the one that produced Cynthia Crawford, the first alien-human hybrid, and many more things I will leave off the page lest I pen a grimoire that might frighten Lovecraft himself. What I can tell you is that the third school is now on other planets in our solar system and has even breached our solar system. It has open communication with extraterrestrial races and partnerships for trade and commerce, a commerce that extends into space what has been practiced on earth forever, slavery. This school is enemy of the saints and enemy of all beings who love the creator and have gratitude for creation. It's in full force now and seeks as its immediate goal depopulation, massive depopulation. If they get their way perhaps one in ten people alive on the planet today will survive. Everything we know and understand about human freedom will be taken away from us.

There is absolutely no need for human beings to go out into space. We've always had the ability to do that just through our consciousness. Ask anybody who diligently meditates. What do you think those yogis in the Himalayas are doing? Do you think they're just sitting in some form of catatonia? There is nothing in space for us as human beings. While we're in the body we're supposed to be concentrating on life here. Put yourself into space imaginatively for a moment. Are you ever going to hear the wind through the trees again? Are you ever going to see a Blue Morpho butterfly? Are you ever going to see the sun rise over the horizon or over an ocean? Are you ever going to hear a mountain stream gently running over rocks? Are you ever going to hear birdsong again? Everything we were meant to experience in a physical body is here on this planet. Space and Satanism are synonymous. Did you not understand *2001: A Space Odyssey* by Stanley Kubrick? There is no life for us in space in the physical form. And now we have a secret space program, and a secret government, and trans-governmental power bodies that dwarf the power of most governments on the planet, and we wonder what's going wrong, and we argue about liberalism and conservatism.

We always imagine this conspiracy taking place somewhere far off in a remote place behind a big door in a room with no windows. The reality is it's taking place right in front of us if you come from a middle class or upper middle class family in the Western infrastructure with people who hold titles. People don't often consider titles. They're an extension of the old titling system of European aristocracies. Their most useful function is the displacement of karma. It's like the human race learned nothing from the Nuremberg trials. We now live in a world where everybody takes orders.

Things never really got better with the old man. In many ways they got worse. As I matured and as I spent more time alone and as I advanced in my spiritual understanding I had less and less inclination to view myself as the problem in the home. I did for some time. The natural inclination of a child is to believe that they were the problem. It couldn't be the parents. All parents love their children, or at least I used to believe that, but it depends on whether the parents have learned to love themselves, or just love in general. It's a terrifying thing to love. There's an inherent vulnerability in it, at least from the human animal survival perspective. But the more years I got between myself and the family, the more I realized I had been severely mistreated, even scapegoated. If I wanted to be really dramatic I could call my upbringing a *soft Moloch* ritual, where Moloch was the demon to which the ancients sacrificed their babies. I wasn't actually sacrificed, but I was treated in such a way that a lot of people might have suicided, either directly and quickly like my grandfather, or slowly through a delinquent life of substance abuse.

I started university at the age of twenty-two. I was a late starter because I needed to get myself set up, apply for loans, and make sure I could do it. As I advanced in my journalism degree my father was near the end of his career as an economist with what we used to call the Ministry of External Affairs. His last big assignment was free trade. He worked for a non-profit organization called the Canadian Exporters Association, but they were in charge of the free trade negotiations. My old man was back and forth between Ottawa and Washington for meetings. The whole thing was a farce. The agreement had already been written and a lot of the meetings were just for show. My old man was little more than a well paid government bag man. I began to have serious questions about free trade. How would it affect Canada? The old man was a vigorous defender of the free trade movement, and like all shit-heels, he gave the same excuse — everybody else was doing it, so we had to do it. Japan was forming a giant trading block in Southeast Asia, and for us to maintain an economy of scale that could compete, we had to enter into free trade.

There's always an excuse with these people. I asked the old man the simplest of questions. What is going to become of the Canadian economy if we lose our manufacturing base? Nobody really had an answer to this question. My brother had already completed a commerce degree from the University of Ottawa, but he was about as bright as a bucket of nails. It's impossible to have real intelligence without spiritual awareness and a functioning heart center. My father and my brother had neither. If you look around you'll see that the world is run by people like this. We throw a title on them, and they get respect even though they deserve less respect than almost anybody in a society — lawyer, doctor, chartered accountant, chartered financial analyst, all licensed professions, an extension of the nobility, the servants of the Queen and London City — and who was I to question the intelligence of this free trade agenda? I was just a problem child who was evicted from the home at the age of sixteen who had now developed, according to the family, leftist tendencies as a result of getting a journalism degree, and this meditation thing, that was schizophrenia according to my mother. How questioning the circular insularity needed for an economy to function and a nation-state to exist is leftist is anybody's guess, and schizophrenia? That was the mistake of trying to share spiritual experience with a woman who flogged herself for god and now worked at a psychiatric hospital. One shudders to think about the people under her care, but once you get a title you're able to label other people. That's what the title is for, don't you know? They're the experts, and we are governed by experts, like the experts who brought us free trade, regionalism, the World Bank and the IMF, and my recent favorite, the mRNA vaccine — experts.

Here we are now, at the end of Western civilization, and largely because of things that were seen decades ago by intrepid journalists who lost their jobs and activists who people laughed at, and people like me, the laughingstock of my family because I dared to question the intelligence of a free trade agreement. As the years went on, I think the old man caught on to what I was saying. He retired in 1992, shortly after the free trade deal. For twenty-five years, as long as his health held up, he and my mother golfed pretty much twelve months a year. They kept a Florida residence and a separate golf membership in Florida, just to golf through the winter. As they aged and their health became more precarious, even the health coverage for a four-month stay in Florida could be ten thousand dollars or more. My father had pulmonary disease, the result of his many years of three packs of filterless cigarettes a day. I remember thinking to myself on many occasions that the devil had learned the human market very well. In Faust a grandiose offer was made for a human soul, but now, in our time, all that is required by the devil is a decent salary and a guaranteed pension. As TS Eliot said, *this is the way the world ends, not with a bang but a whimper.*

Chapter 12

The Letter and the Spirit

The twentieth century was the century of systems, and the twenty-first seeks to lock them in at the level of biology and basic function in the world. There's a strange symmetry to all of it. Cities look very much like central processing units when photographed from above at night. It's like the motherboard and the motherland merged. In North America we got centralized banking in the twentieth century. The US Federal Reserve was formed in 1913 and the Bank of Canada was formed in 1934. People began to slowly experience a subversive indoctrination. Our public narrative was radical individuality and free markets. But the real plan was institutionalization and the perception of an individual as a part of a whole. Both perspectives are accurate and valid for a society to function. It's a false binary antagonism. There are times we have to be part of a collective and there are times that radical individuality is required.

The collective I was born into was the MacDonald clan, the capital city of Ottawa, the upper middle class, the first world, the West, the white race, and the Celtic ethnicity, but all that was taken away from me when I left the home at sixteen. I chose radical individuality, and I have no regrets. In fact, I had no choice. My family wanted to kill me.

All my life I got all my love from within. I tried to express love, but it was too damn hard. Maybe human love is a bit of a scam. Maybe I'm being too hard on myself. Human love is just survival, the survival of our genes through our children, the satiation of our needs for sex and companionship with a wife, and the full formation of the ego through our colleagues and friends. Human love is nothing. Divine love is everything. The way we practice love now in the West — what love — is like the way we do water, portion it into plastic bottles and pretend we invented it.

Throughout my life I encountered high practitioners of many paths to god. I left Christianity behind because my parents went to church, and they were horrible people, phonies and pretenders, always worried more about what strangers thought of them. It's a coward's life. I wanted nothing to do with it. It was like these signposts to god were put in my path. In Taiwan, I met an esoteric Buddhist master. He was also a rotating professor of microwave engineering at Princeton University in New Jersey. One of his students insisted I meet him. I went to his house and he took me upstairs to his temple. I sat on the floor, and he sat on a bench. He told me my aura was blue. He brought in two women, one was his wife and the other was a student. He asked me to read them. I closed my eyes and I told him his wife was clear, and the other woman was blinking in my inner vision. He smiled and asked the women to leave. He then told me the woman blinking in my inner vision was menstruating. I guess I passed some kind of test. He then told me how to breathe properly to affect certain consistencies in my meditation. I was very grateful.

I later met a Taoist master. He and I became friends. We spoke at his home over tea, and, although he gave me no specific instruction it was pleasant to be around him. High practitioners of spiritual arts have an essence, and energy you can feel. You know they're not normal human beings. They keep wind in your sails as you go on your spiritual path. I maintained my base practice, meditation, and I did not deviate from this. Sometimes meditation is just sitting still for thirty minutes or ninety minutes, other times it is a transportation to other realms. The key to these other worlds has always been sound for me. My meditations have been dominated by sounds — the flowing of a mountain stream, the buzzing of bees, the note of a flute, the wind through the Arctic tundra, a thousand violins at once, and things I cannot describe, sounds which have no name. Sounds are the keychain of the universes, realms, and dimensions, and the spaces between, the spaces very few people know about. God left crawl spaces in the walls of the creation.

When I was raising my son in Mississauga I rented a small apartment in the bottom of a townhouse. It turned out that my neighbor was the head of the Mevleviye Order of Sufis. This is the order begun by the poet Rumi. Here's a short poem titled, *I Am Thine And Thou Art Mine.*

> Eternal Life is gained by utter abandonment of one's own life. When God appears to His ardent lover, the lover is absorbed in Him, and not so much as a hair of the lover True lovers are as shadows, and when the sun shines in glory the shadows vanish away.

The sheikh was a radiant human being, touched by god. My son and I danced the zikr every Saturday for a year. The Sufis had a derga nearby. The prayer is tonal. Mantra is not about the words.

It's about the vowels, the sounds we make and hold with our breath. They carry a vibration. They connect us with the above. I was no stranger to the power of sounds by the time I started the Sufi practice. I became a part of the community, as did my son, who was about eleven at the time. He had already developed a great love for the inner life, even as a child. The energy in the prayers was astounding. Everything you have heard about the Sufis is true. After a year I was asked to convert to Islam. I met the sheikh at the coffee shop near my house. I had grown to love the man, as did my son, but we were not converting to Islam. I owed the sheikh my answer face to face. I told him that Islam was the last religion in the world to hold and propel the idea that there was a permanent hell. I told him that the nature of life was more cyclic, as I had already seen many of my past lives in meditation by this point. Of course, even the past lives are something of an illusion carried in the DNA, but that's a discourse I will leave out of this book. No need to confuse things. I told the sheikh that I enjoyed the prayer immensely, and that my son and I felt very much at home, but converting to a religious ideology was not in the cards for me or my son. I added that the permanent hell concept was the fear which generated a lot of the violence in Islam. He agreed with me. The initiates he had with him were speechless at the table in the coffee shop.

What ensued after that was the most epic spiritual battle of my life. It lasted six weeks. Every night when I went to bed something would try to violently pull me out of my body. I grounded myself with breath work. I knew that whatever was on the other side of the veil had no right to be doing what it was doing. I was poked and prodded in my bed, and I had voices speaking directly into my head. A normal person would have been institutionalized.

I knew it was the sheikh or an order of beings on the other side loyal to him. I was never afraid. Never be afraid. Biological fear is normal. Don't try to control your reflexes or nervous system. Let them do what they're meant to do. I'm not telling you to pretend to be some kind of tough guy. I'm saying don't let the fear into your deeper being. Hold your ground and fight. It was an epic battle of prayer and mantra and chi cultivation. On the last day I was outside the very coffee shop where I had rejected the sheikh's offer of conversion. It was there the demon manifested. I was pierced by an overwhelming despair and terror. On the inside my state was like Edvard Munch's painting *The Scream*. I thought I was going to break, and then, into my inner screen tip-toed the Tibetan sage and demon slayer, Milarepa. He was jovial and had a big smile on his face. He roared a giant laugh and the attack ended, and that was the last day of my battle with whatever the sheikh put upon me.

It's not all rainbows and sunshine in the spiritual life. Tests like the one I went through were an initiation. Many initiations are terrifying. Puberty is a biological initiation and the best overall metaphor for what an initiation truly is. It's not knowledge. That's what we get in the stale and dead academe of our time, the passage of information, the memorization of that information. How could an eight-year-old understand the chemical changes and the shifts in thinking brought about by puberty? It's impossible, and that's why the spiritual life has never become public. Our public life has become dominated by the material. If you can't prove it, if you can't replicate it like a scientific process, if everybody can't share it, then it can not formally exist. It's spiritual communism, the comrade partisanship of Satan, his greatest victory in our time, though, to contest the rules today would mean tacitly endorsing the times when we were religiously governed in Europe. It was a disaster. Yet spirituality persists, quietly, in the background, and those being called by the divine are more in number than ever.

I was never able to find a hospitable place for myself in the world. I never bought anything, no house, no investments, no crypto, nothing. I led the life of a devotee. I didn't need to be told what was right and what was wrong. How could it be right to make money on money? How could that be moral? You put no work in the world. I knew this before I encountered the eightfold path of the Buddhist, or Sharia law on economics. How come we had none of that law in the West? My family made money on money. It was one of the benefits of the curse, but it's all ending now. The bullshit that began with the Bank of England, my karmic dowry in this time, my intense and visceral connection to the tensions of Catholics, Protestants, and Jews is all ending. The contract is closing, and when it's over, nobody in future generations will even be able to understand how we got so entrenched in this conflict, so murderous, so Satanic, all of us, not just one group or sect, all of us.

There just wasn't enough inner work in the Abrahamic religions. God doesn't do contracts. It's bullshit. Your life is your contract. The fine print is in every breath you take, every time your heart beats, and every time you show unconditional love for something in the life field, something in the field of god, which goes all the way to the minerals. This contract nonsense has convinced people they're good with God. It's amazing how it just evolved into our commercial constructs — house insurance, auto insurance, life insurance, afterlife insurance — and that's about all the thought people give God.

The Satanists are all about the phenomena, the power, the majesty of the dark entities. If they knew what they were playing with they'd run, but they're stupid. Their time is almost up, and they know it. The most important thing is not to judge them, not to even ask that they be judged. It's not our place, despite what they've done to our governments, our education, our medicine, and our children, especially the children, the only real wealth this human race possesses — no children no race. You can't judge because at the cosmic level judgment is a petition for experience. You have to understand the way consciousness and will work. They want us to judge them. That way we take their liability with the creator. We buy the cosmic version of Florida swamp land.

I've gone light on details in this book, especially with the Carine Hutsebaut material, and there were people she introduced to me, people in this Satanic subculture, who could have been entire books themselves, but I didn't want to write a purely dark story, because nothing is purely dark. I wanted to write a story that lets you know that this has really happened. It's not your imagination. The world is dominated by a murderous cult that sits atop finance, government, the arts, and everything else. We fell asleep at the wheel. We forgot god — our only defense against it — and we're responsible for this multiple car pileup on the freeway of Western society now. It's all real. We've been told the truth at the letter, but at the spirit they've lied to us. This is the way of the devil, and he is an anointed being working for god, and not to be disrespected, nor the demonic legions under him, the princes and principalities, the various forms of non-physical life working with them, and the human agency.

Nothing can happen on this planet without human agency. In the end we were sold out by our brothers and sisters in humanity. Even the devil needs complicit humans to operate in this world. We are the spiritual suzerain here, born through the womb of woman and the seed of man, the contract that starts it all, now soiled and sullied and divested of all sacrament and beauty, and why? To convince us it's better we let them take over procreation, machine babies, science babies, tube babies, genetically modified babies, just like the vegetables nobody wants to eat in the supermarket. That's what they want, and when they get that Satan will have fully stolen the human race from god, but that can't really happen, so the game just gets reset, what they call an *end game* in chess.

The negative is so in charge now, it occupies both sides in the public. It is the good and the bad. It is the ailment and the remedy. Everything is a farce. Everything is a joke. Those forces that stood up on two legs in 1947, those forces that brought us LSD, pornography, money off the gold standard, Charles Manson and other serial killers, MK Ultra and mass mind control, of which digital television is their knockout punch, are running the West now, and it's all been marching to now, the event horizon. The Muslims are correct. We are the great Satan.

It's our lack of understanding about us, about soul, about the supremacy of consciousness that has brought us to this, and of course this was the plan unleashed at the end of the nineteenth century, which brought us the twentieth century, the devil's century, and the sandbox we now call reality. Possession is the normal state of human consciousness now, and even that is a controlled reality. The Vatican is responsible for as many possessions as it alleges to remedy. But demonic possession is not the only kind of possession. There are many dead human beings responsible for what we call mental illness, and there are the extras, things we might call extraterrestrial, extradimensional, and interdimensional. The nuclear explosions brought to us by Oppenheimer and his cabal opened up holes, and things come through holes.

All of my life I kept my spiritual life private. I started having extraordinary experiences from a very young age, so young it normalized itself in my life. It became my normal; prophetic dreams and meditations, sounds and lights in my consciousness as objective as any physical eyes see. There are no voices in the inner life. If you hear voices you've been breached. The spiritual hierarchies speak through imagery and a kind of telepathy. If you gain enough consciousness and control over your dream space you will realize nobody speaks in dreams. You see the person and the messages are received, but there is no speech. It's just that our waking mind doesn't understand telepathy, so it tells us the person in the dream said these things, but there were no voices. I lived a completely normal life, socialized normally, spoke about politics and economics, followed mixed martial arts, and, if asked on a form of any sort my religion, I put down Roman Catholic, my birth religion, but, alongside that normal life I was a voracious consumer of spiritual biographies, holy texts, books on meditation, and I meditated daily, sometimes only twenty or thirty minutes a day, and other times, between work contracts, hours a day combined with long fasts and prayer recitations, either spoken or sung. Why does anyone do this you might ask? Because you experience something, like a drug, and you want more of it. You want to feel this love, this unbelievable unity and connection, and the journeys to other places, which start to take place once you get to a certain level. The journeys are the real hook. They're not physical journeys. They're more like journeys to other realities, realms, and dimensions. They're all around us. You see, the spiritual life is physics at an experiential level. Take away the calculus, the scientific theorems, and all the philosophy of the natural sciences, and you're left with spooky action at a distance as a living reality, not a formula or theory. Once you know this, you know that almost everything we do to progress is a farce, and at first you allow yourself to believe that it's just ignorance, that the intention is good, they just don't know that our body is a launch pad for space exploration. We don't need to build rockets and go there physically, but then it started to dawn on me that it was intentional, that the physical sciences were overplayed, and that it was done to make the spiritual life seem foolish, the province of antiquated dreamers and irrelevant people, that god was not so important as say curing cancer or free energy. If we assume that's true — I do not to be clear — then ask yourself why cancer was so insignificant that statistics were not even kept before the Second World War. So what changed? I don't know, maybe Los Alamos, maybe Oppenheimer and the atomic cabal? And water engines have been around since the middle of the last century. We should have been on hydrogen engines decades ago. It's when you realize it's all a lie, that you realize the devil is real, and his job is to distract us, to keep us in competition, fighting each other, if not over resources then over verses in holy books.

The most fascinating material I came across in the Islamic world, after Rumi and Hafiz of course, was the work of Ibn Arabi. He lived in the eleventh and twelfth centuries and is widely regarded as a saint and mystic in the Islamic world. He is credited with *Wahdat ul-Wujud*, or the *Unity of Being*, a monist doctrine which claimed that all things in the universe are manifestations of a singular reality. He was murdered by Islamic clergy who he accused of stealing from a congregation. And so the world turns. We are all the same. Our mystics are tortured and murdered. Our inner lives are mocked in the new materialist reality, and champions of atheism like Richard Dawkins are cultural voices in the West. You can't get angry, though. They want you to get angry, as John Lennon said, *they know how to handle you when you're angry.* The point is the journey to god is singular, never collective. It will be everything you can do to overcome your own devil, your own curse, your own sin. Taking on someone else's would be like taking on their mortgage atop your own. It's ludicrous. It's always best to keep your spiritual life private, at least until you are so grounded in spiritual experience and reality that nobody can take it away from you.

I find the simple and poor people I live with the best neighbors and friends I've ever had. They don't have any of the bullshit of the big city people, of so-called civilization, yet they maintain a living connection to the oldest and only civilization, life, breath, nature, and community. They work honestly, and they live honestly. I practice my trade of writing in several forms. I did what a lot of experienced technical writers do, I moved into grant writing, it was good money and it paid the dividend of experience. I also write a blog in the artificial intelligence space. I like to help my community when I can, pricey prescriptions, funeral costs, a bag of food in a rough man for a single parent with five children. Being the only North American in this poor community, I'm the only one with money, more than six or seven-hundred dollars a month, which would be a good income on this mountain. Many don't make that. They live on rice and beans, hunt for food, which is only legal for sustenance in Costa Rica. They ride horses or motorcycles. Most of them have dirt floors. My earthbag complex is like a palace up here, but they respect that I built with the earth.

I started to feel the presence of God much more clearly up here. I reject psychic development completely. It's not that I don't experience things beyond the realm of the normal. If you were around me long enough you might come to believe that I'm psychic, but I'm not. Leave those doors closed. Let the belly breathers in the Himalayas tinker with them. There's a difference between divine intuition and being psychic. Divine intuition is a protective space that allows you to know anything that might affect you. It never allows you to pry into the secret spaces of other people. The scriptures are right when they call this necromancy. This nonsense has become the basis of a nearly useless spiritual movement that has emerged in the West, centered on shamanic practices, the utility of plants to experience life outside the body. This is nonsense and just another manifestation of the Satanic force. I've met some names in this movement, and some of them are very psychically powerful. I've watched them fall like sandcastles at high tide when their karma and god catch up with them. God is very patient, and so is the devil, believe it or not. We have to live by certain law. We have to be of certain service to our creator or our lives are useless. Splitting the atom or curing cancer is not being of service to god. Explaining to the human race why we never needed to split the atom and why cancer is so prolific today is service to god. All the heroic nonsense in the Western narrative is just correcting problems we created, a manufactured economy, one side playing the hero and the villain, creating the chaos to provide the order, selling water to put out a fire they started. We put these people up on pedestals. Oppenheimer is practically a prophet of the twentieth century. The question you need to ask yourself is whose prophet is he?

As my parents aged their health turned on them. It's the little things that creep up in the mid to late seventies, then settle in the eighties. If you make it to your eighties, and you live a life considered normal to the West, you're going to have a body to wake up in, but that body is not going to be able to do too much more than just allow you to exist. It's a blessing, though, a holy time in a human life, forced introspection, a meditation imposed. My father hit this forced meditation around eighty-two, then he died at eighty-seven in the middle of 2022. We spoke a fair amount in the last five years of his life. It was the golden age of our relationship, the bookend to the dark age of my youth. We never spoke about the tumultuous past, him casting me to the streets. He did tell me that that was like *another him*, and he did compare himself to Hitler, but he never showed any consciousness of the effect that had on my life, nor did he acknowledge that the family might have perished if I did not allow myself to become the target of his demonic possession, if I did not take the wrath, concentrate his attention on me, confront him that fateful day when I was eight and end the fight with my mother. All that was left off the table. His end years were tormented. The golf was just a distraction. When god took that away and laid him on his back with gradually receding breath due to his COPD he had nowhere to hide. God is merciful, and that's a good thing or none of us would make the cut. My father got a chance to look at himself and atone.

My father was possessed by dark entities that played with his thoughts and took his energy. It's the kind of possession that slips under the radar, the kind of possession that is epidemic in our time, not the dramatic levitating possession of the little girl in *The Exorcist*. That's what they want you to believe possession is. We mask the common possessions with psychobabble from the pharmaceutical and psychiatric communities. But they're liars and profiteers, perhaps the worst example of the exploitative Western economy. If you have your eyes open, and you move around the world a little, you'll realize fairly quickly that North America is the apex of counseling, psychiatric utility, and pharmaceutical consumption. Most societies in the world have absolutely nothing to do with it. I figured out my father was possessed sometime in my mid-forties, when he was in his early seventies. I couldn't tell him. How do you tell somebody something like that? In his mind he was a god-infused man who went to church every Sunday and helped poor souls in church basements at AA meetings, and it's true, he did do those things, but he was still possessed. The possession came from his father, the chain-smoking alcoholic Freemason. These things move in family lines. The Bible explains it well in its own way. When a family is cursed in this way it has to produce somebody who can break the curse. I was elected to do that in my family line, and I have succeeded. Once the curse is broken and the demonic incursion is pushed back, the healing moves out to all the immediate genetic associations, and even to the other side, the deceased in the family line. In the future of this human race, we will understand DNA better, and we'll be able to talk about it as a fulcrum for spiritual expression on the third and fourth dimensions.

As we continued our conversations, my father had a tremendous interest in the things I was writing about. He really enjoyed Stardust Ranch. It introduced him to things he'd never thought about before. I got the sense that he had a tremendous respect for me. It's similar to when you have an adversary your whole life but through continued conflict you come to respect your opponent. It was in his mandated meditation, all that time on his back with controlled breath due to the COPD, that he began to reflect on his life and the inner dimensions began to speak to him. I knew it was happening because he was expressing himself differently. He was seeing the world differently. My mother seemed happy that we were communicating. I spoke to her as well. I never really developed a deep relationship with my mother. I don't think she's capable of deep relationships. She's a very shallow person, despite the suffering she's been through, which began with her father's suicide.

It got to a point in my conversations with my father where he could hardly talk. Sometimes I would call, and my mother would say that he was asleep or resting. This started to happen more and more. My inner voice told me to tell him. I was told to tell him about the family curse and the demonic incursion and that all the voices in his head were not his. I didn't want to do it. Many times the holy spirit will ask us to do things we just don't want to do. What I do in situations like this is I test it. If the impulse does not persist and maintain itself through numerous dimensions, including dreams, meditations, and prayer, then it might just be your ego. It might just be your own inner self telling you to do it, and it's not a spiritual directive. This was definitely a spiritual directive. It got to the point where my father could only speak to me for short periods of time on the telephone, minutes at most. Gone were our long conversations about economics and politics and the state of the world. I completely let him off the hook for his incorrect position on free trade. It had devastated Canada, made it weaker, more susceptible to the dark agenda all around us now. There was no point in rubbing his face in it while he was slowly dying.

In one of our final conversations, he said to me that I was the only child of three who found god, who practiced a spiritual life, and that pleased him very much. As he lay there dying, he realized that god was the only thing that mattered in life. This is a normal course of events for a lot of Catholics. They practice what I call *two minute warning spirituality*, where the two-minute warning is the referees' admonition to both teams that there are only two minutes left in an NFL football game. Deathbed confessions and deathbed repentance are a big part of Catholic culture. Why wouldn't they be? The Catholic doctrine reads like an insurance policy. I told him a little about my spiritual life, how I went through phases where I could meditate and pray for hours a day and I experienced ecstatic states and divine insights. I got the sense he believed me. My mother not so much. She was titled in theology and divinity. She'd lived in a monastery. Whatever happened in that year or so where he was lying on his back for most of the day, the other side got through to him. I knew I was supposed to tell him about the demons, and so I did. I told him that not all the voices in his head throughout his life were his, and that he had done nothing wrong, that these other forces were inherited from his father, my grandfather, and I told him it stopped with me, and his grandson, my son, was protected, and this family curse would continue no more. He thanked me profoundly, and told me that I had *made his day*. He was ready to hear it, and he needed to hear it. My mother was left out of this. We didn't speak to her about it. That was the last conversation I had with my father. He went into the hospital a couple of days later and never came out. He slowly asphyxiated in a near coma over three weeks with my brother, sister, and mother taking turns at his bedside in a Toronto hospital.

I wasn't able to get back for the funeral. It was in the middle of COVID, and I didn't want to get vaccinated. My mother took it very personally. I wrote five-hundred words for the funeral home website, but my sister and mother found it offensive and had it taken down. My mother stopped talking to me after my father's funeral, and I was cut out of the will.

I looked for my father in spirit after he passed. I got no hint of him anywhere. He did not appear in any dreams, and he did not appear in any meditations. It was a full eleven months before he appeared to me in a meditation. In meditation, when my father appeared to me, he asked me if I was going to write a sequel to a book. I had no idea what he was talking about. Three days after the meditative visitation from my father, Robert Wiegand called me up after three years of absence and silence. He said it was time to write another book. He said I had to tell my story, tell what I knew about darkness and light. I said okay.

That's the story of my family curse. I had to wait for my father to pass for the curse to lift. It was like he was grounding the evil to the earth, and because of our genetic association it had access to me. There are people out there now in the spiritual community who are saying they can lift trauma. It's nonsense. This life we live is gridded in ways we will never understand. We must accept what it is to be human. I have seen many miracles in my life, true miracles, conceived and deployed for me and me alone, constantly reminding me that the divine is a real presence in my life and in everyone's life, whether they realize it or not. Be wary of the people selling miracles. It's getting increasingly difficult to tell the good from the bad, the spiritual from the diabolical, the takers from the givers.

My father was born on the second of June, as was my son. At the time of his conception his mother and I had broken up as girlfriend and boyfriend. I had not seen her for several months. She passed me on the street in downtown Toronto and did a U-turn. We spent an afternoon together and my son was conceived. My birthday is July twelfth. I was born forty days after my father's thirty-first birthday. My son was born forty days before my thirty-first birthday. As I said, we all live in a big grid of time, space, event, destiny, and fate. Nobody really understands it. The Satanists try to hack it for material benefit while they're incorporated in the body. The religious pretend it doesn't exist. Spiritual people know it exists. We honor it is a part of life and use the insights we gain to further our commitment to the divine and service to the human race and all life on the planet. This is the way.

Spirituality is simply about creating time to be silent and aware without the mind and the senses. It's really that simple. I know this isn't going to stop anyone from doing decades of research in the same manner that I did. The thing about this science, the spiritual science, is that you cannot rely on the work of your predecessors because it is such an individual science in which the canvas of proof is within us, it is not a shared science, but it is a science nonetheless, the science of spirituality.

My wife in Costa Rica is a Christian. She's also died twice and come back. I find myself here on the mountain returning to my first teacher, the Christ. The gospels are uniquely powerful and uniquely true. I don't meet too many people actually living them though. It's too damn hard. I had to find god in a circuitous way. That's why it's so curious that Christ comes back to me at this time of my life. Don't get me wrong, I don't believe in salvation doctrine. I don't believe in a spiritual credit system where simply by saying aloud — like *Abracadabra* — that you believe in the Christ that your sins are forgiven, you're going to go to paradise. It's just not that simple. My mother and father were wed to Christ their whole lives and went to mass at least once a week. The curse was never lifted off of them. We have to live what we've created. I don't want to get into a long dissertation on reincarnation here, so let's just stay with the idea that the sins of the father are inherited by the sons. Let's stay with the Bible. God was the ability to cope with the incredible weight put upon my shoulders. My spiritual work did not lift the curse.

When you look at the state of the world today, don't put all the blame at the feet of those people who attend the rituals at the Mother of Darkness Castle in Belgium and locations like it all around the world, including Canada and the United States. They're certainly the dark end of the spectrum, but the real reason the state of the world is so abysmal now is all the quiet people who don't stand up for their values, who don't live the words of the Christ, or live them only on Sundays, or only when it suits them, but never when it interferes with a guaranteed income and pension. If that's the line you won't cross in service to God then you are as much a part of the problem in this world as the people who go to the rituals. They would not be able to do what they do without you working for a police service, a mercenary military, a predatory Treasury Department or Ministry of Finance, and of course, the most diabolical culprit of all, the center of the octopus of control, and the de facto family business for my father and brother, the banking and economic system that has taken over the world. The problems of this world are nowhere near insurmountable. In fact their childishly easy to resolve. It's just that we do not get leaders who want to resolve the problems. We get leaders who perpetuate the status quo. We get leaders that are pretty much placed in power by the invisible power brokers we never see.

I love my family. It all broke apart when my father passed. My mother took in the darkness that had been living inside my father when he passed, and she is very dark now, a horrible fate for a woman of eighty-five, but we get exactly what we deserve in this world. The sooner we understand and accept that the sooner we can be released from the sins of our fathers.

Afterword

I would like to thank all the people who helped me write this book. First and foremost there's Robert. Without his guidance and support this book would not have been possible. How such people even come into an existence is still a mystery to me, but they do. I'd like to thank my wife for her constant support and the cultivation of a space in which meaningful work can be done. Lastly, I would like to thank Anthony for coming along for the journey of this book and editing chapter by chapter and providing a sounding board for what was coming out. What I learned in this journey is that one doesn't really find God. It's more like God is always there. The job is cleaning out all the debris and garbage in our minds and in our hearts that block God. We have to fight our demons. There's no other way.

About the Author

Bruce MacDonald was born in Ottawa, Ontario. He has a journalism degree from Ryerson University in Toronto, Ontario. He is the co-author of the non-fiction works *Stardust Ranch: The Incredible True Story* and *The Light of Darkness: A Warrior's Tale for our Time*, as well as the literay fiction *The Stolen Child* and *God is an Economist*. He works remotely as a technical writer in the fields of software and telecommunications from the Province of Limon, Costa Rica, where he lives on a small farm in the Talamanca Mountains with his wife, Rosemary.

Printed in Great Britain
by Amazon

58472926R00149